Old Madam Yin

Old Madam Yin

A MEMOIR OF PEKING LIFE
1926–1938

Ida Pruitt

Stanford University Press
Stanford, California

Stanford University Press
Stanford, California
© 1979 by the Board of Trustees of the
Leland Stanford Junior University
Printed in the United States of America
Cloth ISBN 0-8047-1038-4
Paper ISBN 0-8047-1099-6
Original edition 1979
Last figure below indicates year of this printing:
89 88 87 86 85 84 83 82 81 80

INTRODUCTION
By Margery Wolf

Ida Pruitt was born in China in 1888, the daughter of American missionaries, and spent the first twelve years of her life in a village in the province of Shantung. In these formative years, she developed an understanding of things Chinese that matured into a rare appreciation of her adopted culture. She came to America for an education, gained experience here as a medical social worker, and then returned to China. From 1918 until 1938 she was head of the Social Service Department of Peking Union Medical College Hospital, a job that allowed her to blend her two heritages in service to her adopted country.

In Peking she lived in a way that revealed the depth of her dual heritage. Her home was Chinese, and she says of it in this book, "One's house is very important. It is the third and outermost of the shells that encase us. We do not choose our bodies, but we care for them and adorn them. We choose our clothes and our houses with regard for their fitness. My house, though many times smaller than [Madam Yin's], was as traditional in its layout, as well-built, and as harmonious in all its levels of roofs, its proportions in the houses and courtyards, and its details." The friends Ida Pruitt invited within her outermost shell were both Western and Chinese, and her ease in both cultures was a service to both. One wonders how many Westerners in those twenty years were aided by Pruitt in their first steps toward understanding the unique beauty of Peking and its inhabitants.

Fortunately for us, Pruitt has extended these good offices far beyond the few dozen Westerners she met and befriended in China. Through *A Daughter of Han*, first published in 1945, generations of students have come to appreciate the quality of life among working-class Chinese without becoming mired in sentimentality; they have also been introduced to the despair of poverty in prerevolutionary China without the politically motivated exaggerations that raise doubts about those realities. In her new book, *Old Madam Yin*, Pruitt tells us of a way of life that will never be found again in China, that of the very wealthy. She preserves for us the style and grace of their world without either romanticizing them or castigating them for a lack of social enlightenment as yet beyond their comprehension. She also gives us rare glimpses into Peking's foreign community—another class of people and way of life no longer seen in China—during those last years before the Japanese occupation. But for the China scholar, the value of *Old Madam Yin* derives from Pruitt's keen eye and expert control of ethnographic detail.

The Chinese family system was organized around the kinship of men. The ancestral rites performed in the lineage hall focused the patrilineal principle and celebrated the antiquity of the male line. Be he mythical or real, the founding ancestor was always male. Women were the property of their fathers' and then their husbands' lineages, but they became members of their husband's lineage only after death. Men were born members of a lineage. The birth of a daughter who could not provide sons for her father's lineage was treated as a disappointment at best; the birth of a son—even one with a multitude of elder brothers—was cause for feasting and celebration. This cultural imbalance is reflected in much of the scholarly literature on China in that the lives and activities of women are barely touched on. Ida Pruitt's books are a rare exception. Without lecturing, she shows us how *women* viewed Chinese society.

When a feminine perspective is taken on a male-oriented society, the conflict between gender stereotype and reality becomes starkly apparent. Chinese women were weak of body and character, incompetent in the world of affairs, and dependent by nature. Anyone who remembers Ida Pruitt's Daughter of Han and her women friends will find the stereotype ludicrous. Before Ning Lao Tai-tai learned the ways of the world outside her walls, she might have preferred to live quietly at home raising her children; but once necessity forced her out into that world to make a living, she did so with zest and skill. She learned quickly what people to see and how to motivate them to act in her behalf. Too often women's political skills are unobserved or discounted because they operate in arenas that are not public. Ning Lao Tai-tai, however, did as well as any man in her social class when it came to accomplishing things in the "world of affairs." If this woman was by nature dependent, she concealed it remarkably well.

Among wealthy women it is harder to see beyond the stereotype, but once again Pruitt has allowed us to wander behind the spirit screen. Although Chinese decorum insists that women must obey their fathers and brothers when young, their husbands when married, and their sons when widowed, Old Madam Yin, a very decorous lady, was a thoroughly independent personality. She loved her children, but she had learned, as every woman must, that the system worked for men and that men may or may not bestow their assets equitably. In an attempt to control some of the uncertainties life held for women, she built a row of apartments to provide for the education of a granddaughter. Knowing the predilection her son had for his second wife over his first, she adopted a son for the latter and built another row of apartments to finance his education. This was neither dependent nor incompetent behavior. Strong character in Chinese women is recognized and admired only when they are old and is attributed to the fact of their age. But if they were dependents and incompetents before their hair turned white and their husbands died, how did they suddenly acquire the skills and attributes necessary to dominate a household? A careful reading of Pruitt's books will answer that question and pose another: How did we not recognize half of the population of China for all these years?

In the last decade some anthropologists have suggested that men and women operate with different models of the social and symbolic world. Pruitt's studies of Chinese women suggest a less sweeping interpretation, namely that women simply reject some of men's social constructions (such as the sanctity of the male line in China) and adapt others to fit their own understanding of women's capabilities. Madam Yin gave an example when she showed Ida Pruitt and three friends a painting of Mu Lan, a young woman who went to war in place of her elderly father and returned home with military honors. " 'A good filial daughter,' Lao Tai-tai said piously, but the gleam in her eye told us that women could do anything they put their minds to whatever their country or race, and that the implied compliment to the four foreign women from the hospital had not been the only inspiration of her remarks."

An apt example of the adaptation of male models to female needs comes from *A Daughter of Han*, and it uses the very imagery of the male ancestral myth to illustrate the strength and power of women. Speaking in a somber mood brought on by her educated 35-year-old granddaughter's failure to marry, Lao Tai-tai says, "Life must go on. The generations stretch back thousands of years to the great ancestor parents. They stretch for thousands of years into the future, generation upon generation. Seen in proportion to this great array, the individual is but a small thing. But on the other hand no individual can drop out. Each is a link in the great chain. No one can drop out without breaking the chain. A woman stands with one hand grasping the generations that have gone before and with the other the generations to come. It is her common destiny with all women." Many times have I heard men expressing this sentiment in Taiwan, but never once have I heard one suggest that the crucial links were female. It was not a topic women dwelt on, but when this old woman who had been cut adrift from the men's family system wished to place herself and her children in the larger context of society, she turned not to her husband's family (although they all bore his surname), but took the model of all men's families and identified the links in the construct as female.

Ida Pruitt is not interested in anthropological theories. Her purpose here is to share with us her intimate knowledge of the lives of Chinese women, teaching us to appreciate as she has their subtleties and strengths. For me the ultimate test of Madam Yin's character was in her chance meeting at Pruitt's house with Ning Lao Tai-tai, the working woman of *A Daughter of Han*. Seating arrangements in China, even at a foreigner's tea table, are matters of rank. On this occasion Madam Yin neither assumed her own right to the higher place nor deferred hypocritically to her social inferior. Instead the two women dueled with great humor and energy over the honor of taking second place—both of them far too intelligent to pretend to ignore their difference in rank, both far too genuine to think it really mattered. In this her ninety-first year, Ida Pruitt has added another personality to our cast of notable Chinese women and another dimension to our understanding of Chinese society. We are all in her debt.

Old Madam Yin

CHAPTER 1

It was because Lao Tai-tai (the Honorable-Exalted) wanted a grandson that she had come to see me that first time, and it was because we became friends that we continued to see each other.

It was necessary that the Wife of the Second Master, Lao Tai-tai's Second Son, should have a son. The concubine was young and beautiful and pregnant. It was not fitting that the eldest son of that branch of the family, in the House of the Second Master, should be the son of a concubine; and the Wife should have her own son to cherish her in her old age and to worship her and take care of her needs after she should have joined the ancestors.

These things were told me by Li Kuan, the social worker who made the routine visits to the families who wanted to adopt children from us. Babies born in our hospital were healthy and well nourished, and our fame had gone abroad. We were able to find good homes for those who were not wanted.

"The Wife is about thirty-five and has a daughter of twelve. She has never had any other children. There is no hope for a son from her. She is sick most of the time. And—" Li Kuan lowered her voice in respect, "her father was a famous scholar. His family did not have much money but everyone knows about it. It is one of great renown."

This I realized was an added reason there had to be a son for the Wife. The Yin Family would have had much public opinion against them if they used ill the daughter of a famous scholar; and if they went further than necessary in being good to her, they would build up much prestige.

Li Kuan read my mind. "It's not from fear of public opinion that they think of adopting a child but because it is the right thing to do. Lao Tai-tai has a kind heart and she knows what is fitting. She is the head of the Family—has been since the Old Master died. I guess she was that before also—and she wants everyone in the Family to have what is right for them to have. There is the Family responsibility to the daughter-in-law."

I saw that in Li Kuan's mind the decision had been made. She felt we should give a child to this family. "But," I protested, "they are rich. That means the child will be cared for by maids. He will be the pampered pet of a lot of women and be utterly spoiled. You know our policy. We do not give babies to wealthy families—where the mothers themselves do not care for their children."

"But this family is different—" Li Kuan refused my generalization.

I smiled. I knew her enthusiasms.

"It really is different. They have not always been wealthy, and the women of the family are like the women we know in the families of our friends. They live very simply. And—" Li Kuan hurried to get away from the subject I had raised, "you should see the house. It is as beautiful as the Imperial Palace in the Forbidden City. And you should see—"

"From what is their income? Who works at what?" I brought her back to the subject.

"They have a family estate in Anhwei Province, from where the Old Man came. The First Master, the Eldest Son, cares for that."

"So they are absentee landlords living in the city off the rents of the land."

"Oh no," Li Kuan hastened to say, "the estate is not large. It supports only the First Master and his branch of the Family. It is the Second Master who counts. He is the one who has made the money. He ran a uniform factory in Mukden for Chang Tso-lin, the Old Marshal, and he came to Peking with the Young Marshal. He now runs a uniform factory here and he has other businesses besides." Li Kuan was trying to hurry past this topic. She knew that I did not like the uniform factories and the pittances they paid the women who worked in them from daybreak to sunset. We often saw the women pouring out of the big gates at dusk, eyes glazed with weariness, looking straight ahead and seeing nothing but the home toward which they doggedly walked; and knew that they clutched in their hands what should have been barely enough to feed themselves but without which they would have had nothing to feed anyone. Why did the industrial revolution, taking women's work out of their homes, give them always so little and ask for so much, when it first came into any older pattern of life?

"He has a wonderful collection of paintings and ceramics." Li Kuan knew my love for the beauty of China, its physical beauty and that made by its men and women of genius and that made by its ordinary people also. "The Second Master is the Head of the Family here in Peking. He is the one in the family who makes money. The Third Master is teaching in Tientsin but he comes home often. He has one of the courtyards in the compound. The Fourth Master is at school in Paris—"

"Then the family is one of real wealth." Only a family of wealth could have sent a son to school in Europe or America, unless on a scholarship. I was sure Li Kuan would have mentioned the scholarship had there been one.

Li Kuan's eyes looked faintly distressed. "They are wealthy now but they have not always been so. They are simple people like us." Then, as though that clinched the matter, "The Second and Third Masters went to school in Japan and the First Master has never been anywhere outside the country." It took less money to send sons to school in Japan than to Europe or America. The financial condition of the family could be charted by the schooling of the different sons. She went on quickly to allow me no time to think of more questions. "There is also a daughter still at home."

Then Li Kuan drew a deep breath. "May they come to see the babies tomorrow?"

My office was invaded next day. A silken flood poured into

3

the room. Like an army with banners flying the family invaded the room, with Lao Tai-tai, the general, in the van. I began to understand many things.

She did not hesitate in the doorway as most callers did—for effect, out of formal courtesy, or waiting for directions—but started immediately across the room toward me. There was no jar of the harmonies in the room, no breaking into the pattern, but the rhythm of the room swung wider and the accents shifted.

She walked swiftly on her tiny bound feet—no more than six inches long—bound beautifully according to the fashion of footbinding of the North. She came across the room with a speed and grace that made those of us with natural feet look as though we moved in sections.

She was a little over five feet tall and was slender as a mature woman is slender. Her coat, cut straight as all coats were cut for both men and women, did not hang flat but showed shadows. Her coat and trousers were of grey silk—the grey of which the Chinese are so fond, the grey with life in it. A pattern of tiny twigs woven into the cloth caught the light and heightened the sense of its life. Her clothes were cut in the modified "old fashion" that had great style and distinction. The coat was wide and came to her knees. The long sleeves were straight and wide. The trousers were bound in at the ankle above the little triangle of starched white cotton stockings and the tiny black cloth shoes. The narrow straight standing collar buttoned around a firm neck. Her grey hair was combed back into the conventional chignon on the nape of her neck—"modern" yet Chinese, uninfluenced by Western ways. Her face had been "enlarged"— the hair plucked from the forehead on her wedding day to straighten the hairline and make the high square forehead that was the sign of a married woman. Her face was smooth and could have been the face of a young woman but for the wear of experience that showed, not in any wrinkles, but in the lifting of the planes and the heightening of the cheekbones. It was an oval face, wider at the top, but enough off the classic symmetry to make it arresting—the cheekbones were too high and one was very slightly larger than the other. The eyes were long, with the deep fold and the double lids that were so highly prized. They must have been very beautiful when she was young and were still very fine. It was the expression in the eyes, however, that was most arresting. There was joy in life, zest in life and in all things of life. There was a vibrancy in her whole person that seemed to go from her toes to every hair lying so smoothly on her head. She was a complete person, in harmony with herself and her world.

She sat on the chair I offered her, the one by my desk, and sat bolt upright. She did not touch the back of her chair, and yet there was no hint of strain or effort. She was as relaxed and graceful as though lounging—which I was sure she never did—in her own garden.

Li Kuan made the introductions. The bevy had sorted themselves out according to precedence and were seated around the room.

"This is the Second Mistress." That would be the Wife of the Second Master, the one who would be the mother of the child about to be adopted. Her well-bred face, though not pretty, was well enough formed, but had the flattened-out look so often seen in the faces of women who are not loved, those who do not fight the frustrations of their lives. With spirit her face might have been distinguished, though it could never have been beautiful. She wore the long gown-dress of the current style—a modification of the Manchu robe. The dull dark material was rich enough but seemed muted to meet her muted existence. She seemed older than her mother-in-law, even though one could see easily that she was a woman in her thirties.

"This is the Second Young Mistress." The term Li Kuan used was that for one born in the house and not for one married into it. This then was Lao Tai-tai's own daughter. Somewhere there was another and older one. The daughter would have been addressed by the same title whenever she was in her mother's home even if she had been married, but the long heavy braid of black hair down the girl's back had already told me that she was not, and her likeness to Lao Tai-tai had already told me whose daughter she was. She was vivid but still not as vivid as her mother. I felt I was seeing something of what the old lady must have been in her youth. The girl's long black silk gown—she was still in modified mourning for her father—was cut with as much style as her sister-in-law's lacked and was worn with the grace the other woman had never had.

"This is the daughter in the Second Mistress's House." The girl of twelve was shy but was also interested in watching what was happening. Something, apparently, of the Yin spirit had descended to her.

"And this is the Third Mistress." I looked at the tall, gaunt woman whose like I knew so well—no ideas, no charm, just a woman of the leisure class, the wife of the Third Son, the Third Master.

The serving woman, standing unobtrusively but not at all withdrawn, was not introduced.

Lao Tai-tai leaned forward. "About that baby for me—that I may take my grandson home—"

Inwardly I gasped. This was most unusual directness. She did not talk of the weather or the meals we had eaten, or ask about my health or family tree. She did not need this period of sparring to work out her plans, nor did she need it to sense the situation. All was settled in Lao Tai-tai's mind, and I could see why all was settled in Li Kuan's mind also. I was to learn that she was always direct and also that she had already taken my measure as I had taken hers.

So the silken wave flowed down the hospital corridors and into the small ward where, temporarily, we had four of the babies for whom we were finding homes, and engulfed the four cots. There was for a while the sound only of soft cloth-soled shoes sliding and patting around the beds, and through the hospital odors of milk and drugs and soap floated a faint fragrance of sandalwood and musk.

None of the others said anything while looking over the babies as women look over goods in a shop, but they watched the old woman out of the corners of their eyes. Methodically she

6

went from bed to bed, asking me at each to tell her the background of the baby that lay in it. We did not give names or details of the families they had come from but told of the kind of stock from which each child had come. Whether the child had come of farmer stock, or student stock, or from the poor of the city was considered to be of great importance. Some liked best the "clean country heritage." Others were pleased to have a child whose parents were intelligent, were students in the universities of our great city. The Old Lady stayed longest by the bed of a well-developed child of eight months. He had a "long-square" face, a well-shaped head, and well-marked features already showing the good bone structure beneath. Fortune tellers—those who tell the future from studying the features of the face and the shape of the head—always prophesy success and official rank to those who look the way this child did. He also gave promise of classic beauty.

"And this one?" Lao Tai-tai asked as she stood by his bed.

"His mother was a serving woman, and his father was the master."

"Ah—a secret child. Look at this forehead, the shape of his head. He is a well-put-together human being. Secret children are strong and intelligent."

I knew of this belief. "His mother is a very intelligent woman," I said. "I have never met his father."

"He has a bad temper," said the nurse, standing by the bed, dressed in her starched white uniform with the little starched white cap on her head. "He knows what he wants and yells for it."

The others had now gathered around the Old Lady.

"This is the one we want." Lao Tai-tai's voice was completely assured. It was evident the decision was hers to make and not for the one who would be the child's mother. "We'll take his eight characters and let you know as soon as we have had them read." But I felt sure from watching her that the geomancer, the Master of Wind and Water, who read the "eight characters" (two for the hour of the child's birth, two for the day, two for the month, and two for the year, and all out of the mystic cycle

7

of the Ten Heavenly Stems and the Twelve Earthly Branches in their endless revolutions of sixty and then another sixty) would watch her face even more shrewdly than I had and, unless he saw something positively malign in the horoscope cast from these "eight characters," would read them to suit her.

Lao Tai-tai came several days later to sign the papers and make the child her grandson. As she was leaving she turned to me and said, "I'll get him a wet nurse. I'll start looking for one right away."

"But he's eight months old," I said, "and able to eat many things. He has learned already to drink out of a cup. You can get powdered milk for him and we'll give you a list of the things he may eat."

"Has he ever been on the breast?"

"No. He has had the bottle since he was born."

Straight as Lao Tai-tai was standing, she stood even straighter. "I'll get him a wet nurse. It is not right that any human being should not have had the experience of sucking at the breast."

Lao Tai-tai was the only member of the family who came the day the new grandson was to go home. With her was a tall young woman, broad of shoulder and with full breasts pushing out the flat surface of her short blue peasant coat. She had the large-sized bound feet of the farm woman whose feet had been allowed to grow until she was eight or nine years old, or even ten, instead of being bound at five or six as were the feet of the girls from families of wealth. After all, she would have to do heavy work in the house and on the threshing floor even if she did not go into the fields except to carry the noonday meal to the men as they plowed or reaped, or perhaps to glean after the wheat harvest. She carried a bundle wrapped in a red cotton cloth.

With one of her quick movements Lao Tai-tai took the bundle from the young woman, untied the knots, and one by one took out the red silk garments—little split trousers of red silk lined with red cotton, an underjacket of red silk also lined with soft washed red cotton, a topcoat, red shoes with tiger-head

8

toes, and the red tiger cap, its ears decorated with tiny silver bells that would tinkle every time he moved his head. The only things not red were the diapers of soft, much washed, old blue cotton. Lao Tai-tai handed the garments to the young woman, who dressed the young lordling as Li Kuan, the ward nurse, and I stood by and watched. Last of all was the bright red quilt that wrapped around him as the young woman took him up in her arms, to follow the old woman out of the hospital.

Lao Tai-tai was taking the Young Master, her grandson, home.

CHAPTER 2

Li Kuan and I were both disappointed. She had hoped to show me the glories she had told me so much about in the house, and I had hoped to see into yet another of the mysteries of Peking, to see beyond yet another of the great gates breaking the walls that lined the streets and hutungs (the residential streets) of the city. There was, I knew, endless variety within the pattern in those compounds guarded by the great gates and by the spirit screens inside the gates and shielding them. Credited with keeping ghosts and demons from entering the compounds and wandering through the courtyards and houses, the spirit screens effectively kept out the peering eyes of those who passed on the streets. The line of vision, like the demons, moves only in straight lines. The party had been at night and we would not have been able to see much anyway. Also since they seemed to regard us as mere acquaintances, it is doubtful if they would have shown us around. That, at least, was the way I explained it in my own mind.

The occasion was the Completion of the Month party given by the family for the new grandson. It was the custom in all families to celebrate the birth of a son with feasting, to entertain the relatives and friends when a new son had been in this world a month and proved that he could survive that long. It was the introduction of the new member of the family to the relatives and friends. The new grandson had been with the Yin Family a month and must be introduced to their world even if he was nine months old instead of one.

Lao Tai-tai had come to the hospital herself to give us the invitation and tell us how well the child was and that his name was to be Ken—Root or Foundation. He was to be the foundation for building the Second House of the Yin Family, the one that was the most vigorous. "I'm inviting you for six o'clock dinner so you can come after your work," she had said.

Li Kuan's face said as plainly as words, "They're pushing us off, inviting us for the tag end of the day and making out it's for our convenience." In a family of such wealth there would be feasting all day. Would not the important guests be at noon? But after all why should they not push us off? There was no reason why the Family should be more than courteous to us. They might even wish not to be reminded that Little Root was adopted.

We were entertained in the outer reception room. In all traditional Chinese homes of many courtyards and many houses there is one row of rooms opening onto the Entrance Court, the court between the Great Gate and the Second Gate. In this row of rooms the master of the house entertains those of his men callers who may not pass through the Second Gate, the gate into the family quarters. This is also where he transacts his business. A big table had been set up in the central room where the ten of us—Lao Tai-tai and her guests—sat. With traditional courtesy Lao Tai-tai urged us to eat, but her gestures were stereotyped. She was somewhat bored herself. The food was that served by restaurants for such occasions, good but uninspired, a set menu. We were obviously among the odds and ends being cleared up. The relatives and close friends had been feasted during the day. The other guests with Li Kuan and me were a nondescript group of women, none of whom I ever saw again and none of whom made any impression on me. I could see also from Li Kuan's sulky face that she was not only disappointed but aggrieved.

From time to time Little Root, in the arms of his strapping wet nurse, was brought in and exhibited to the company. In spite of being so well wrapped up in the red quilt and in spite of the distraction of the red coat and the tiger-head cap with its tinkling silver bells, we could see that he had grown in the month and looked well. This however did not satisfy the company.

"He looks well. His face is round."

"Can't tell from the face. Sometimes the face is round but the body is quite thin."

"The real test is the back."

"The back—"

The wet nurse knew what was expected of her. She had already been loosening the quilt. After all, was she not proud of the flesh she had made with her own rich milk? She let the quilt fall apart and turned the little lordling over on her arms and flipped up his coat to show, between the halves of the so very sensible and convenient split trousers of childhood, the pair of rounded cheeks like a full moon shining on the company.

"Ah—" The women all let out their breath. "He is fat and fair, fat and fair."

We were glad that etiquette allowed us to leave—in fact required us to leave—as soon as the meal was over. It had been served rather rapidly, another proof that we were among those to be paid off and not among the really favored guests.

We had played our part, had been feasted, and, I felt sure, would soon be forgotten. I had reckoned, however, without taking into account the qualities in Lao Tai-tai I had seen in my few dealings with her but had not realized were so highly developed. One was her determination to get the best of anything to be had that was needed by her family, and at the lowest price. This quality she shared with all her countrymen, but the degree of energy and skill she brought to the game—and game she and they all make it even when most serious—was her own. The other qualities were her love of people and her vibrant curiosity. These also she shared with her people, brought up in that ancient culture. She brought to them, however, more energy and imagination than did most. And besides, as the family made no effort to keep the adoption of Little Root secret she could see as much of us in the hospital as she chose.

The best medical advice in the Western pattern was to be had in the hospital where Little Root had been born and where Li Kuan and I worked. We had been at great pains to impress this on Lao Tai-tai, hoping that the child could be seen through the difficult years threatened by measles and mumps, scarlet fever and diphtheria, and wrong feeding—seen through these years by our specialists for children. Also the best medicines were to be had in our pharmacy, as well as that difficult to be obtained and expensive American product, powdered milk, for Little Root's supplementary feedings and perhaps also for the Third Master, who smoked opium. It was well known that opium smokers could drink milk when they could eat nothing. Everyone knew the best prices could be got through the intercession of the Social Service Department.

Lao Tai-tai could see no reason why she should not benefit from the reduced rates we could get for our patients, and if not free, as for the poor, at least with a discount. Was not the relationship between the Social Service Department and Little Root that of parents to a child? Had not the child come from our department? Even if we were no longer the child's parents, could we not at least be counted his "outside grandparents"? Would we not want the child to have everything he needed? The ethics governing the treatment of family members were involved. Did one not always strive to get the best for one's family and one's friends? Did not relatives help each other? Was that not part of the responsibility of life—the other side of privilege, of the equation, the rule by which good men lived: Every responsibility has its privilege and every privilege has its responsibility?

I do not think that Lao Tai-tai ever understood why we could not give her free or at a discount the supplies she wanted. There were several thousands of years of agricultural-handicraft society behind her in those ethics, as they had developed and served the people, to give weight to her reasoning. The world was made up of families, and it was the duty of every member of every family to get all he could for his family and for the friends who then became honorary family members and were treated as such. Furthermore, was not the source of all good things, the great broad earth, open to all who could seize her, and did not the more able get more of all good things for their families and so ensure the continuation of those families?

Whether one was rich or poor was determined by Destiny. It was part of Destiny to be born with ability to get things and to have ancestors buried in the places that could influence for good the fortunes of the family. It would be going against the gifts of the ancestors if one did not use one's ability to get all one could for one's family. Even Destiny would not work if people did not fulfill their destinies by using the abilities and opportunities they had.

Lao Tai-tai accepted my word, however, that we had to charge those who could pay. There was nothing else she could do if she wanted to buy from the hospital. Even paying our full price, what she wanted from us was still less expensive than if bought in any drugstore or grocery of the city and certain also to be of good quality. As we became better acquainted she knew that what she had sensed was true—that there was no lack of the friendship relationship between us but only that strange foreign way of doing things. She could not understand, for she did not know the pattern of the ethics used in the hospital way of doing things, but she had the faith in me to see that I must be acting according to a pattern, and the intelligence to accept what was inevitable. How was she to know the ethics of relationships that science and the machine were demanding of the world, that had their roots in other continents?

These things were not said. They could not be said by either of us. But they were in her mind and in mine. We saw them in each other's faces. We knew there were areas in the mind of each, deep in those minds, that each did not understand of the other and that each sought to understand. I had the advantage of having been born into both the patterns and therefore knowing something of the way her mind worked; she that of being steeped in one of the patterns, according to whose precepts she lived.

She came to buy milk powder for Little Root and to buy cod liver oil and vitamins. She came to get medicine for the servant seen in the surgical clinic. She always came for one thing at a time, and she always came to my office and sat, back straight, on the edge of the chair by my desk and chatted gaily and with wit. To give her face I would go with her to the drug department and chat with her while her prescription or order was filled and go ceremoniously with her to the outside door.

One day as she sat by my desk she began to laugh. I had picked up the outside telephone and then the house telephone as they rang insistently, and sat with one to each ear. People—members of my staff, patients, messengers with notes, doctors—had been coming and going, interrupting our conversation. She laughed and leaned forward as I put the telephone down. "I like you," she said. "You and I are alike. We both like people and we both like to have a bustle going on around us. Also we both like to manage other people's affairs."

The phrase she used—managing other people's affairs—like so many things had its good and its not so good meaning. It could mean a busybody and was often used in that sense: "Why are you interfering in what does not concern you?" But it also meant a willingness to be helpful and neighborly, to go the extra steps beyond those required by duty, and a keen curiosity. I was sure she was not calling us busybodies, and that she should interpret the work of the Social Service Department as being helpful and neighborly was satisfactory to me.

"I like you. Will you visit me at my home—have tea with me?"

She saw the answer in my eyes.

"Come early so you can see my gardens. And would you like to see the house? Bring friends with you. You know I like people. Bring a lot of your friends."

CHAPTER 3

On the day appointed four of us got into the motor-car we had hired and drove to the North City. The three friends I had selected carefully for the privilege and honor of seeing behind Lao Tai-tai's spirit screen and of sharing, for an afternoon, Lao Tai-tai's friendship had been chosen as people who were interested in the ways of other peoples as well as their own, who were not aggressive, at least in their manners, and who could be counted on to conduct themselves with a certain amount of restraint.

The adventure started, as all adventures in Peking started, as soon as we set foot outside our own gates. The streets of Peking were a never-ending pageant. Furthermore, we were going north, going to a part of the city where we did not often go and should see things we had never seen before. We wondered what we should see in those streets we knew and yet did not know.

It was a wonderful day in early spring. The air was like crystal to the eyes and flowed into the lungs like clear spring water down a dry throat. The strips of red paper with the bold black characters brushed onto them—bits of poems—that had been pasted on the gates at the Chinese New Year had not yet completely faded, and the branches of the trees lining the streets and spreading over the walls from inside the courtyards no longer looked brown in the sunshine. They were pliant and sent out gleams of green and yellow. The blue sky stretched cloudless into infinity and the golden sunlight turned the dust on the old stones of the pavements into yellow crystals, as though fresh yellow earth had been spread for an emperor's chair bearers to tread upon.

The four giant arches—the Eastern Four Pailou—that straddled the road where two of the main streets crossed, looked as they always looked, as though their red legs were carrying them forward, as though they were marching, eternally marching, while they stood on guard on those wide Peking avenues. To the left was Pig Market Street. In the early mornings the squeals of a thousand pigs could be heard from its inner reaches as they were carried to the place where they were made ready to feed Peking. To the right was Grain Market Street. Through the open shop fronts could be seen the sloping bins full of the "five grains" that were the food of the people—glistening white rice, soft brown wheat, tiny golden beads of millet, sturdy round green beans and brown flat soya beans, and purple and white kaoliang (sorghum) grains. Among the grain shops were the Mongol shops, where, if we hunted, we could find the narrow strips of heavy Tibetan woolen cloth, wine red, white, or yellow, with a tie-dye pattern of crosses in blue or white. We could, if we were fortunate, find Mongol saddle rugs and boots and holy pictures from lama temples.

Beyond the Four Pailou, where we had crossed the main east and west streets, we began to count the hutungs, the residential streets. The First was where the Language School—the College of Chinese Studies, where Western students learned to speak and read Chinese—was located; and the last turned east to the Russian Mission, established in 1685, in the time of the Emperor Kang Hsi, when he brought to Peking the Albazin prisoners his troops had captured on the banks of the Amur. Somewhere between was the great Lama Temple, the Yung Ho Kung, where the ceremony to drive out the demons for another year was held every winter and where every day the lamas, dressed in their long yellow robes, could be heard chanting their prayers in their very deep voices. If we had gone west on one of the hutungs we could have seen the yellow roofs and pine groves of the Confucian Temple. But we turned east on the Fourth Hutung.

We passed the back of an old temple with roofs of black glazed tile—the landmark we had been told to watch for—whose Ming Dynasty bricks were undisturbed even though the protecting plaster had fallen from their sides, the mortar from between them was wearing away, and the lichens made patterns over them.

I murmured something to the chauffeur about going a little more slowly so I could watch for the gate. Li Kuan was not with us, and as I had been once only before and then in the dark I was not too sure of recognizing it easily. He seemed to think, however, that a dashing approach was needed. I was not surprised therefore to find the Eastern Wall of the city looming before us. We had missed the Yin Family gate. After an argument the chauffeur consented to take us to the little police station to ask the way. His whole attitude told us that we were making him lose face—that we should have known the way, or at least have a servant along to do the asking.

The police box, of pine boards painted black, nestled against a well-built, white-plastered wall. The policeman, in his black cotton uniform with the white puttees, came out of the little wooden structure and spoke to us courteously. "The Yin Family? Which Yin Family?"

"The Yin Family with a Lao Tai-tai (an old Mistress) and several young Masters. They live in a large compound. There could not be a second family with so large a compound in this neighborhood."

"Ah—this would then be the family of whose garden this would be the wall," and he pointed with his chin to the wall back of his sentry box. He had known from the first question what we were after but had spun out the conversation in order to see us all, take in what we looked like, so that he might tell his tale to his cronies when he was off duty. Why should we begrudge him this interlude in his eventless day in this far corner of the city?

"But the gate?" we persisted. "Where is it?"

"Ah, the gate. It is there," and he pointed to the street corner a few yards away.

The market streets and thoroughfares of Peking and the hutungs are laid out at right angles and with great precision. They flank the Forbidden City on the east and on the west. Between the Forbidden City in the center and the walls of the whole city the streets and hutungs bisect solid blocks of compounds with their courtyards and houses surrounded by their own walls. Between this solid tree-grown grid-work, where people live and work and play, and the city wall there must have been wide spaces left when the city was given its form in the fourteenth century by the early Ming Dynasty emperors. These were parade grounds where the troops who manned the Gate Towers, who guarded the city, could drill and march and maneuver. As the character of fighting changed and troops no longer shot arrows from battlements, and as the dynasty grew weaker and the bannermen no longer left their barrack villages, houses began to creep out into the open spaces. The ends of the hutungs, once sedate and controlled, frayed out like the ends of ropes. We had passed, at an angle, the end of the street where the Yin Family Gate was located, had come down another street, and had therefore not seen the servant standing on the steps waiting for us. At Lao Tai-tai's request my cook had telephoned to Lao Tai-tai's gate-keeper when we started. He was surprised to see us coming from the east instead of the west.

The gate was wide open, and the man who stood on the steps was in the long blue cotton gown of the servant on duty. Seeing us he ran back into the gate and came out again followed by another manservant, one with more dignity, age, and presence. The gate-keeper had called the steward, or perhaps it was the assistant gate-keeper who had called the gate-keeper. We were being welcomed in formal style. This then was the reason Lao Tai-tai had made such a point of our telephoning ahead about the time of our arrival.

In the brief moment before the gate-man opened the door of the car and ushered us up the steps, I looked at the length of the front wall of the compound as it stretched to the west—for the gate was, as it should be, on the eastern edge of the property—and saw from the roof lines that it was several courtyards wide. Set in the walls were blocks of wood with heavy iron rings where the horses of the visitors of the past had been tied while their masters feasted inside. There seemed something undignified in the way we had to crawl out of the car into the dust of the street instead of alighting from a cart drawn up to one or the other of the "step off the horse" stones that flanked the steps to the gate. But the car was too large to reach them. That we had adequate face, however, was made clear by the steward as he led us up the wide flagstone steps stretching the width of the Great Gate, giving plenty of room on each wide shallow lift for dignified and stately walking.

The "gate-cave," as in most big Chinese compounds, was a *chien* or unit of the front row of houses, of the house that backed the street, whose rooms opened into the Entrance Court. To set the gate off, however, from the rest of the row and to balance the steps, the roof of the gate section had been raised, and it had its own ridge pole and finials. The two big heavy black-lacquered wooden leaves of the gate hung by wooden pivots. They could close against a heavy wooden threshold, high enough to be a bench for children and old servants, across the middle of the cave. They were now hospitably open, both leaves back against the wall, making the whole of the gate-cave into one room which was also the passage.

Just beyond the threshold, in front of a little door on the east side, stood an old man with a few grey hairs on his chin. His long blue gown, his dignity, and the fact that he stood in front of the door that could be to no other than the gate-keeper's room told us who he was. A gate-keeper was always an old and trusted servant. He had great power in the household. No one could get through that Gate without his permission. The tips of the guests were his main income, and in a family that entertained largely the income was not small. When, a few years earlier, telephone service had come in, the telephones had been installed in the gate-keeper's room, where he could control all messages. No member of the family ever touched the instrument. Telephone calls were made by one's secretary or servant to the gate-man, part of whose duty and privilege was to receive the messages and relay them as he saw fit. A telephone conversation could take twenty minutes or half an hour, or become hopelessly bogged down if he did not approve. The position of gate-keeper in a big household was one where a man could fill his pockets if the family was active and many people came to visit. Positions of gate-keeper to great families were highly prized posts. They were the honorable pensions given to the most worthy servants, and posts also that could be held by the old.

Across the inner end of the gate-cave were six or eight narrow wooden doors painted light green, each swinging on its own pivots. They could all be shut at once and, even if the Great Gate were open, block all view into the compound. They were all open today to let us in, had been taken off their pivots; but I knew that usually the one at the west side would be open to let the family come and go.

Across the Entrance Court, built into the wall, was the Spirit Screen. In lesser homes this was a small detached wall standing just inside or outside the gate, to block all direct view into the compound. Here it had become an ornamental facade of polished brick, with a pattern in the center of carved peonies, flanked by geometric designs, completing the balance and harmony of the main entrance. The privacy of this family was fully guarded. Even when the two leaves of the Great Gate were open and all the leaves of the inner gate removed no one in the street could have seen into any but the Entrance Court or seen anything but the Spirit Screen. To give this added security to the privacy of the home was the reason the Great Gate was on the east end of the front wall of the compound. Never should a gate be in the center. If it should be in the center and open, and all the doors in all the houses and the gates between the courts were open, there would be a view down the whole length of the conventional compound. What family could stand such an invasion of its privacy? What family could stand the flood of evil spirits, those beings who traveled only in straight lines, that this would let in? "Only an Emperor had a destiny strong enough to withstand the ills" that could come sweeping in. His living quarters, however, were guarded by a series of throne halls and walls to the throne hall courts between his living quarters and the Great Front Gate. This gate was the front gate of the whole city and also of the Forbidden City, his home. It was in the center of the wall, but the gate in a private home had to be on the eastern side of the front wall. The front gate must be on the east because "A man turns his face to the east." I was constantly tantalized by phrases and ideas half expressed, passed down by tradition and not always understood by those who passed them down; and by the suggestion that a house, like a suit of clothes, like the body itself, was another and outer shell for the chrysalis, the essential person, whatever that might be.

The steward led us down the steps into the long narrow Entrance Court and turned to the west. On the north we passed the traditional Second Gate, which led into the family quarters, and on the south the row of rooms which backed on the street, where we had been entertained at Little Root's Completion of the Month party. We went toward a moon gate in the west wall. From my experience with other compounds this should have led us into the library courtyard, where the master of the house had his study and where he entertained his friends.

Most compounds were built on the classic and traditional pattern of three axes. In the Forbidden City, the home of the Emperor, the Empress who lived in the courtyards and houses of the East Axis was the Empress of the East and the one living in the courtyards and houses of the West Axis was the Empress of the West. In temples, the houses on the courts of the central axis were the main halls of the main gods. In the courtyards of the eastern and western axes were the smaller shrines to the lesser gods, the quarters for the priests, and the courtyards where travelers could stay. In my old home in Shantung Province, where the home of a wealthy family had been turned into a mission station, all the houses were on the central axis. The east and west axes had become walled walks. In my own house in Peking, a middle-class house, the two side axes were represented by narrow spaces behind the east and west houses of the main court. These spaces made possible small high windows in the back of the houses and so achieved cross-ventilation. In a compound the size and grandeur of Lao Tai-tai's, however, I was sure the traditions would be fully followed and the axes complete. To see therefore instead of the library a very stylized formal garden was a surprise. I learned yet again that within the formal pattern there could be a great variety, and that this one though traditional was not typical. Even as I was to find that the family was not typical.

A brick path laid in the "everlasting pattern," the pattern that has no beginning and no end but goes on forever, led through a maze fenced by braided bamboo strips. Flower beds, newly dug up and prepared for planting, were between the low fences. Across this garden we went through a gate into another court. This I realized was the library. An open gallery ran around the brick-paved court. Set in its walls were the painted glass fronts of lanterns shaped like fans, vases, and peaches. They could make a gentle light for an evening party. Potted oleanders and pomegranate trees had already been brought out from winter storage and lined the path across the court, their tiny leaves just beginning to burst red from their coverings. From the ridge poles I could see that the house before us was a double house such as was seen sometimes in temples and palaces. The grey tiles flowed over the front house roof without a break, while the roof of the back house was finished off with a raised ridge pole and upturned finials.

Lao Tai-tai stood between the pillars of the railless verandah before the house, welcoming us. Behind her and to either side, as though standing casually but with due regard to the family rank of each, stood her daughter-in-law, daughter, and granddaughter. Little Root, in the arms of the wet nurse, was just behind and to one side of Lao Tai-tai.

The steward was able to be both humbly behind us and graciously in front. He ushered us across the court and up the steps, and then he was holding up the heavy padded door curtain of winter. It had not yet been taken down to make way for the bamboo curtain of summer. We were ushered into the house, through the entrance chien, to the west, into the formal reception room. My heart sank. Were we after all to sit in leather overstuffed furniture, such as we could sit in in any hotel or club? Why should the polished brick floor be covered with a rug, even a heavy Peking rug? It should be bare and easily swept clean of the shells of the watermelon seeds that might drop and the dust.

But I should not have worried. This was the formal and correct way to receive guests. Lao Tai-tai had to carry out the ceremony of greeting her guests even though she was as anxious to be active as we. She talked, as we sipped the "fragrant leaf" tea, about the weather and Little Root's new teeth, as a preliminary only. As soon as good manners were satisfied, she sprang up and asked, her eyes sparkling, "Would you like to see the whole house?" And I knew that the gardens and courts were always counted as parts of the house.

She led us into the entrance chien again, and I saw more clearly the heavy red-wood table and the two chairs of red wood flanking it on either side. They were in the formal position opposite the entrance door. Lao Tai-tai pointed out the open beams and rafters whose beauty Li Kuan had so much admired and whose green and gold and red I had been looking at as we sat, whenever the conversation had not needed me. The little scenes painted on the beams were as dainty and the colors as strong and pure as any in the Imperial Palace itself. There were old scholars in their pavilions, bunches of wildflowers, lotus blossoms floating in ponds, gods in the Western Heavens—

The wall separating the entrance chien from the room beyond was of carved hardwood shelves filled with books. The books, wrapped in covers of brocade or of blue cotton, lay on their sides, ready to be taken out from either room. Their bone or ivory fasteners made rows of highlights.

We could see that the room beyond was a scholar's study. There was a traditional scholar's desk against the north wall. On it were the usual scholar's tools—the pen holder made from a section of bamboo, and with a mountain scene carved delicately on it and filled with brush-pens of many sizes; the slab of stone on which the scholar ground his own ink; and the stick of solid black ink itself. The water container for making the ink

24

was a collector's piece—a little bronze peach. I wished I knew more about these things. I knew that every scholar put great thought into their selection. Back of this study was a small retiring room with a large couch where the scholar or his friends could go for a nap or a whiff of opium, or to recover from his drinks if he felt he was beginning to have too much. A Chinese rarely allows himself to become drunk. The wall between these rooms was another set of shelves of carved hardwood.

"Look! The patterns on the two sides are not alike." Now that Lao Tai-tai pointed it out to us we could see that the vines and leaves curving around the bits of china or jade or bronze on the shelves curled in one pattern on this side of the shelves and in another on that. Yet the bits of art could be seen from either side and could be enjoyed at the same time by those in the study and by those in the room behind. Lao Tai-tai beamed. She was proud of the skill that could execute such a tour de force.

A dignified man in his late thirties had come into the house while we were looking at these things. He was dressed in a long gown of sober-colored woolen cloth, and his hair was cropped short like that of any city gentleman. Lao Tai-tai introduced him, "The father of Little Root."

He had come in through the back door, from the court where, we were soon to learn, his wife lived, the mother of Little Root. The harmony of life, the Chinese know, is made up of many rhythms that must blend and supplement each other if there is to be any happiness and peace. It was not fitting that he should have been among those who first welcomed us, for we were a group of women visiting the women of his household. It was fitting, however, that he should meet us and thank us for his son. It was also fitting that he should not wait until in the tour of the compound we should reach that part where he was living with his concubine. And it was fitting that he should approach us through the quarters of his wife. Whether he lived in her quarters or elsewhere, it was fitting that before their friends he gave her the honor of the Wife. Furthermore, the son for whom he was thanking us was his Wife's. There was no rigid rule for the blending of these rhythms. The harmonious results came from estimating with skill the varying pulls of all the principles involved.

That the Second Master was in his middle or late thirties and his wife about thirty only and their daughter twelve added weight to Li Kuan's story of the family's simpler beginnings and rise to wealth. In families of inherited wealth the sons and daughters usually married early. In the old families of landed gentry the boy was often only fifteen and the girl eighteen when they married. Both boys and girls in city families of wealth were usually married when they were seventeen or eighteen. This pair seemed to have been married when the wife was eighteen and the Second Master in his middle twenties. This suggested that perhaps at the usual time for marriage the Yin Family had not had the money to make the kind of marriage they wanted for their son. This difference in age might have been due, however, to his waiting until he returned from school in Japan before looking for a wife.

The Second Master's features were regular, the face a little longer than round and with no one feature outbalancing another. His back was straight, showing that whether he was educated or not he was not one of the old literati who cultivated a scholarly stoop. He looked more like a competent and not undistinguished man of affairs.

He greeted us and thanked us for his son and then answered our questions about the bits of art on the shelves, telling us the periods of the ceramics and the kinds of glazes used at the different kilns and the special points of interest in the jades and bronzes. When we complimented him on his erudition he smiled and said, "It is not large. These things I have only just begun to learn." Whether this was the self-deprecation demanded by good manners or the truth we were left to guess. I was inclined to think he was telling the truth and that having lately reached a position of wealth and some leisure he was only now taking up the scholarly pursuits that befitted a gentleman.

Lao Tai-tai again claimed our attention. "See this door? It

looks like a mirror if turned this way and the other way like a framed picture." Lao Tai-tai swung the panel in its frame. "Do you know the story in this picture?" It was that of a warrior of the old feudal period about to mount his horse. Both were decorated with plumes and the warrior was in armor. A servant held the horse. "You see we too have women who can do things," she said with great satisfaction. "This is Mu Lan." Mu Lan was a maiden who had gone to the wars in her father's place when he had been called up by his feudal lord and had been too old and too ill to go himself and had no sons to do this duty for him. Mu Lan had fought successfully through the required period and returned home with military honors. "A good filial daughter," Lao Tai-tai said piously, but the gleam in her eye told us that women could do anything they put their minds to whatever their country or race, and that the implied compliment to the four foreign women from the hospital had not been the only inspiration of her remarks.

The little room beyond this door was piled high with hardwood chests, some carved and some plain. "Full of pictures and scrolls of calligraphy," Lao Tai-tai said. "We take them out and hang them—some of them—at New Year time." She opened a little carved wooden box with sloping sides that was sitting on top of a chest and began to show the long multicolored scrolls it held. They were those that told of official rank—given to an official by the emperor when he was appointed to a new post. In the center were stamped the huge imperial seals, six or seven inches square, one in Chinese and one in Manchu, side by side. I had seen these many times elsewhere and so freed myself to look at the picture on the west wall.

This picture covered the wall from cross beam to floor and was so large that the white parts of the scroll on which it was mounted had been rolled up at top and bottom. It was in black and white—a scholar's picture. It was of a woodland grove. A couple of scholars were in the lower lefthand corner, facing inward on the path that led up into the grove. They were placed strategically for Chinese perspective. I could go with them as they walked through the grove, getting ever deeper, until away off in the far distance of the upper righthand corner they disappeared with the winding path. So strong was the suggestion of the picture, so deftly did the path lead the eye ever deeper into the grove, it was a shock to see the two little scholars still standing in the lower lefthand corner, walking deeper and ever deeper into the grove. The spirit of peace and harmony spread from the picture to all in the room and flowed on and beyond.

Unwillingly I heeded the gentle pressure—Lao Tai-tai and her son standing, waiting by the open door for me to pass—to leave. I could not, I knew, spend the whole afternoon in front of that one picture.

We went through the back door (all back doors were on the west end of the house) and found ourselves in a courtyard paved with fieldstone that had been polished by the rains of many years. Trees were at either end of the five-chien house across the court, and there were flower beds under the windows. The Second Master himself lifted the door curtain for us to enter the house, and when we looked around he had disappeared. This was the house of the Wife, Little Root's mother, but he did not live here.

We sat in the central chien, in the stiff hardwood chairs, and drank more tea in honor of Little Root. His twelve-year-old sister handed around a lacquered tray with six moveable sections holding nuts and watermelon seeds, sugared green plums, Hami-melon, and coconut. She smiled shyly at us with the engaging shyness of the young Chinese girl which becomes the charming feminine smile in the Chinese young woman. In neither is it a shyness that has any fear; rather it is the shyness of a person who will not reveal all at once but waits until there is a relationship of give and take, retreat and advance, where there can be an ever-growing and deepening emotional tie.

The house in the courtyard to the east was closed. This was where the Third Master and his wife lived when they were at home. They were now in Tientsin, where he had a post in the Customs Service. This courtyard was back of the maze garden through which we had passed on our way to the library.

Between the Third Master's courtyard and the maze garden

was a pavilion which looked as though it were built of bamboo, but as we came closer we saw it was made of wood carved like bamboo. Light and graceful, it was part of the garden, patterned I imagined after the tea houses on the banks of the lakes or on the islands in the lakes of the region "South of the River" (the Yangtze) whose beauties had for centuries been sung by poets and painted by artists. Lao Tai-tai pointed out that the lattice of the windows was of the cracked ice pattern.

"This is where my sons and their friends will sit to drink tea while they savor the fragrance of the flowers and make poetry," said Lao Tai-tai, but when we went into the pavilion we could see that no one had yet sat there to drink tea or make poetry. There were still shavings on the floor, and the one or two rattan chairs looked as if they had been brought to be mended and as if the workmen had been there not long before. This might be the first year there would be flowers in the garden—so new everything looked. "I think my Fourth Son will be the one to like this best."

Why was this house so new when those in the other courts seemed to be old—so lived in and settled they looked with their deep foundations of large burnt brick and heavy dressed stone. Perhaps the original pavilion in this garden had fallen to pieces, as buildings of such light construction were apt to do.

Lao Tai-tai moved on. "Come," she said, "and look at the maze." We threaded our way through the windings and turnings of the pattern, the "Everlasting Word," that potent word embroidered on their garments, engraved on their stones, woven in their cloth and laid into their pavements, the word, born of the sun and the wind, that crosses itself and goes on without end, that cannot end. As we walked along between the low bamboo palisades we listened to Lao Tai-tai talk of the flowers she was planting and knew that the garden would be a poem when in bloom. This was the garden of the flowers that had to be planted each year. Already there were little shoots appearing, and plants had been brought from the greenhouse to some of the larger beds. "These plants are as much trouble to me as children. Morning and evening I must see to them." Lao

Tai-tai laughed in delight. "My children tell me I work too hard over them, but what do they know?"

"Come up the hill," she said when we got to the south end of the garden, and she led us up the artificial mountain of rocks and earth piled against the street wall. "The women who lived here in the old days could not get out as we do, and this was the only way they could see anything of what was going on outside. The men liked to sit here too in the cool of a summer evening and catch the breezes." We followed her up the brick and stone path that wound around the rocks, as the Pilgrim Paths wind up around the hills to the great temples, and through the tiny valleys until we reached the little square pavilion with open sides, on top of the highest peak. We sat on the round stone stools around the stone table and looked into the street, and thought about the funeral and wedding processions that would have brought the women of the household here in the old days. They would have heard the horns blowing and the gongs beating and have come up to see the many-colored banners, the sedan chairs of red and green and gold, or the catafalque. Perhaps they sat here to watch the dances given by the different guilds during the month after the New Year, or in the Fifth Moon, when they went on pilgrimage to the temple on Miao Feng Shan—the Mountain of the Mysterious Peak. There would be lion dancers, swooping with their green and gold heads and tails of paper-mache and bodies of painted cloth. There would be stilt walkers dressed in long embroidered robes and elaborate headdresses to represent the Immortals. There would be sword dancers with their red sashes and baggy black trousers. They would be parading through the streets from the temples where they practiced and where they kept their gear and their god. These things we could think as we sat on the stone stools and imagined ourselves women of the past. The twelve-year-old granddaughter looked around curiously. Perhaps she had not been up before. She had no such need to peep at the world from afar as she would have had if she had been born to this house a few decades sooner. She went each day in her own rickshaw through the streets and hutungs to a modern school.

Across the street a block of unfinished houses lay like a sharp black-and-white pattern—so dark was the grey of the new tiles and bricks and so white the new plaster—set in a wide-stretching pattern of light browns and greys where the dry earthen walls were peeling and the bricks and tiles decaying. There was something wrong with that black-and-white pattern. Its lines did not flow with the rhythmic harmony of the courtyards and houses in the old compounds around it but were harsh and rigid like a grill, the houses and courtyards of equal width. Also the wall between the road and the compound was too low. It was high enough, to be sure, to shut out the sight of the courtyards from the people walking on the street, but we should not have been able to see the windows and doors of the houses from where we were. We should have seen the roofs only, as in the surrounding compounds.

New and old, they were all houses for the poor. They were all low and the courtyards small. They all faced south as all houses should and therefore all got the healing, cleansing sunshine, but these houses with the narrow courtyards between the rows would have no privacy from the sight of the neighbors except when the windows and doors were shut (which could not be borne in the heat of summer) and no privacy at all from sound, so close was every neighbor, a family to a room. I had counted six doors opening into the court, so close together they could open only into one room each. Six doors! Six families!

"Houses built for rent," I said to myself. "No one who intends to live there himself would build so closely." The houses of one middle-class family around a courtyard could have fitted comfortably in that new compound, and the whole of it could have been put into one of Lao Tai-tai's courtyards. I noted, however, that the tiles and bricks were new and the walls well-coped. They would not melt with the rains of summer as did many walls every year in Peking. The landlord-builder was one who looked into the future and not at immediate gain only, one who was building for a long-term investment. The tenants would at least be dry.

"I'm building these houses for my granddaughter. They're to put her through college." Lao Tai-tai smiled gaily.

Why after all should I expect Lao Tai-tai to go beyond the pattern of the way of life in which she had been brought up and in which she lived? Why should I expect her to think of people outside her family, her own circle? Was not her duty to get all she could for her own family and those who belonged in one way or another to her family? Were not all others "outsiders"? After all, "Within the Four Seas all men are brothers" was the lofty concept of the most idealistic of China's scholars. To how many people anywhere in the world was it a part of what made them think and act?

And the thought crossed my mind, "She is still afraid of the concubine's power over her son, afraid that his money—and he is the one in the family who makes the money—will be used for the concubine's children. Lao Tai-tai is taking no chances. She is making sure herself that her granddaughter, even though she is that son's daughter, will get an education and have a dowry."

As we repassed the Bamboo Pavilion, Lao Tai-tai again spoke of her Fourth Son. In her mind it evidently belonged to him. Perhaps she was planning it to be his living quarters. I wondered how she would furnish it. "He's in Paris, you know, studying law. He will be graduating and coming home this summer." Through all the restraint of her breeding there still could be felt the pride she had in him, her baby son. I wondered about the relationships in this family and would have wondered more had I known more of what they were.

Back in the Third Master's court—and I noticed that Lao Tai-tai scarcely ever mentioned him—we went forward through a gate into a courtyard with a "rockery," a little rock mountain, perhaps ten feet high at the central crest, on one side and a wall broken by two little gates on the other. This court was back of the Main Courtyard, the Master's Courtyard. I could see the back of the Main House to the south of this little rock mountain, its ridge pole highest of all in the compound.

"These stones came all the way from Yunnan Province. It took us months to get them here. And there are not many men alive who know how this kind of rock mountain should be built. We got the only man in Peking who knows how to build one. It was in ruins when we came—when we bought the compound. We had to repair it and buy new rocks."

I wondered why there was a rock mountain behind the Main Courtyard and the house of the Main Courtyard, but when Lao Tai-tai turned north, away from the rockery, and started for the first of the little gates saying, "This is the Hall of the Ancestors and that," pointing with her chin to the other little gate, "is the Hall of the Gods," I understood. I thought of Coal Hill behind the Forbidden City, the home of the Emperors. It too was an artificial mountain, between the quarters of the living family and the ones devoted to those who had joined the ancestors. Instead of the three crests of this little mountain in the home of a private family, Coal Hill reared its five crests, each surmounted by a pavilion, high behind the imperial home. It guarded the Emperor and his family from all untoward influences coming from the north that might sweep in on the cold north winds, from those malignancies that lurked where the sunshine could not find them, and from those that might come from too great use of the added strength whoever had passed on might have gained. North of Coal Hill were the halls where the imperial family kept their ancestral portraits and tablets, seats for the imperial spirits to return to at the stated times when they were welcomed and worshiped by their descendants; and the halls where the bodies of those who had joined the ancestors lay in state, awaiting the auspicious days for them to enter their Earth Palaces. Back in one of those little courts toward which Lao Tai-tai was leading us, the one on the right I was sure, Old Mr. Yin had waited many months for the auspicious day for him to enter his earth home, until his grave was ready for him. Li Kuan had told me that. It was necessary to separate the quarters given to those living in the Western Heavens from the quarters of those who still lived on earth. Although the line between the living and the dead was very shadowy, a mere matter of not seeing, it was necessary for those who had passed over to understand that they should return to visit their relatives only when invited. This little "rock mountain" was the dividing line as well as the protection.

Lao Tai-tai led us through the gate into a little courtyard and across to a small house built like a temple. She pushed open the red doors with white paper pasted on the latticework of the upper halves, and we saw on three tables against the three walls three perfect little wooden houses of finely carved wood—three shrines. The one against the north wall, opposite the door and so in the place of honor, was about four feet high and the other two were slightly lower. Each was a little temple of carved wood. The curved tiles on the carved roof were held up by carved rafters seeming to hold up the overhang. As in all houses and temples there were latticed windows across the front of each little shrine and latticed doors that hung on pivots. Before each tiny doorway were incense burners, candlesticks, and plates with offerings of fruit and cakes, tea and rice. The ancestors must not lack food in the other world. Lao Tai-tai lit a bundle of incense before each shrine and made a curtsey as she placed it in the burner before each door. "The three generations of those who have gone before"—these were the generations each family was required to worship. There were five generations that each man hoped to be able to venerate—his father and mother, his grandfather and grandmother, and the three generations preceding them.

I knew that Lao Tai-tai's husband, having died before her, was automatically higher now in rank than she and that if she had died first she would have been higher now in rank than he. I knew that she must therefore burn incense to him as did her sons. I knew that his soul tablet, with the little drop of red ink that symbolized the drop of life blood on it, was now in the western house, the shrine against the western wall. For he was of the latest generation to pass over and must occupy the house lowest in rank. A shadow crossed Lao Tai-tai's face, and I wondered if she were thinking of how much she missed the one to whose soul seat she had just offered incense. In each little house were several tablets. I could not see clearly into the dim interiors and so could not tell how many wives Mr. Yin's father or grandfather had had; nor could I tell if there was another tablet already in the shrine with the Old Man's.

Lao Tai-tai's spirits were much lighter as we went into the courtyard of the Hall of the Gods. This also was a little temple against the back wall of the little courtyard, with a weeping willow hanging over the low building.

Opposite the door as we entered, on the table, was a glass shrine housing a bronze figure of the Buddha of the Future, every fold of his fat flesh neatly executed, a beneficent smile curving his fat lips. There was an incense burner, a plate of fruit, and another of cakes before him. On his right hung a picture of Kuan Yin as a beautiful woman, the bringer of mercy, and on his left was one of Maitreya Buddha. Lao Tai-tai lit a bundle of incense and set it in the burner on the table, but it was clear that she was not much interested in these deities. She gave Kuan Yin a half-approving look and turned to the east. I had no opportunity to see what was on the west wall, for Lao Tai-tai called us over. "This," she said with a beaming smile, "is the best of all."

"And who is this?" I asked, for I did not recognize the scholarly-looking old man in the picture hanging on the west wall, the little old man with the intelligent, shrewd face. He was sitting in a garden with a great tree behind him and flowering shrubs around, dignified in his long flowing blue silk robes and tall black hat of a long-past dynasty.

"He is the Second Son of the King of the Fox Fairies. He was so good and learned that he was allowed to take human form. We worship him for scholarship and for official position and for wealth." These, I knew, were synonymous to most of the people. She lit a big bundle of incense and set it in the burner on the table.

Outside again, I saw—what I had not noticed as we came

35

in—an inconspicuous gate beside the back of the Main House. A low roof with a chimney from which smoke curled could be seen over the low wall. I guessed the door led to the clan kitchen. Lying on the ground in front of the door was a long dirty greyish-yellow mop. Suddenly it stirred and rose a little from the ground. Barks emerged from the tangle, but it was impossible to tell from which end.

Lao Tai-tai laughed at my surprised face. "It's a Tibetan lion dog."

One of the maids had by now picked up the creature and brought it over, growling, for us to see. The long, honey-colored hair hung over its face and merged with the long honey-colored hair growing down its sides, hanging almost to the ground. The tail was long and bushy and, in this specimen, usually between its legs. "He has not the least bit of courage," said the maid.

"When his mother has puppies again you shall have one," said Lao Tai-tai. She had seen my collection of Pekingese dogs and knew how much I loved them.

There was a wisteria arbor back of the east end of the Master's House. The vine was still brown and looked dry, but I could imagine it with the great purple clusters cascading as they would in a few weeks.

"I often have breakfast here," said Lao Tai-tai. "I like to eat wherever the fancy strikes me." She saw me looking for the chairs and table that Westerners think necessary for taking food. "I sit on the ledge," she said. And I could see her sitting cross-legged on the wide dressed-stone ledge of the foundation that ran around the house, about a foot and a half above the ground and about two feet wide. The maid would bring one of the flat thick mat-like cushions—or perhaps Lao Tai-tai would bring it herself—and a tray with the bowls of steaming food would be placed before her. Meals must be lonely for her now that the Old Master had passed over. Each unit of the family— each son and each wife of each son—had its meals to itself. Lao Tai-tai was too busy a person to try to adjust any of them to her times and seasons. Perhaps she had started having breakfast under the wisteria vine while the Old Man lay in state in the House of the Gods behind the wall shaded by the bamboos. Sitting there she could watch while the servants carried food and drink to him three times a day for the many months he lay there, until the time came for his burial. I could see Lao Tai-tai watching to see that he was served before she ate herself and burning incense before him. "I like to hear the rustle of the bamboo while I eat," she said.

Lao Tai-tai led us toward a little gate in the east wall. "We are going to my Second Son's house," she said. The Wife and daughter had disappeared, and I could see Little Root's wet nurse carrying him back toward his mother's house.

"My Second Son lives in a foreign house."

"How dreadful!" I thought to myself. I had visions of the monstrosities that had been built in some of the Peking court-yards—great square blocks of brick and concrete without form or comeliness. Heavy two- or three-story buildings with star-ing glass windows, they sat—undigested lumps—in the gra-cious courtyards behind the noble gates. But I need not have worried. The man who modestly disclaimed any special knowledge but had selected the pictures and bits of art we had seen in the library could not have perpetrated anything as dreadful as I had feared. As we passed through the little gate we saw a low building with a low glassed-in verandah in front. It was essentially a Chinese house; only the closed-in verandah made it "foreign." Also it nestled among the trees and shrubs instead of having an open court before it. But was that neces-sarily foreign? Did not the garden houses in any palace com-pound appear and disappear among the trees? I could see that we were now in the Great Garden, the Gentlemen's Garden, the garden that was beautiful all the year around.

The Second Master himself held open the screen door to the verandah and greeted us. Then he turned to the woman stand-ing a little to his right and back of him and told her to greet the guests. Lao Tai-tai, who was courteous as always, gave the young concubine the title that was hers by courtesy only and murmured to us, "My Second Daughter-in-law."

She was young, no more than eighteen, perhaps only the sixteen she was rumored to be. A result of intensive training in the arts of pleasing men, her sophistication could well have added a couple of years to her looks at this end of her life but—if all went well with her—could give her many more years of youthful looks at the other end of her life. She was one of the most beautiful women I have ever seen, and the price of her redemption from the "House of the Wide Gates" must have been very great. The black hair drawn back from the face formed a smooth shining helmet fitting close to the head and was done in a traditional knot at the nape of her neck. The face was the traditional apricot seed shape, with the broad forehead and pointed chin. The cheekbones were not high as in Lao Tai-tai's face but just high enough to give a play of light and shadow on the planes of her face. Her skin was fine and smooth, the color of white satin that has been kept a few years but glowing with the color sent through by her young blood. The eyes shaded by the heavy double lids were bright and black; thanks to the folds at the corners of her eyes, they looked like elongated almond seeds. The eyebrows had been plucked to the shape of willow leaves and seemed ready to flutter away. The face, vibrant in its living stillness, was alive like the face of every woman who is loved, perfection given to what was ready to be perfect.

She was many months pregnant. The Wife had not acquired her son any too soon if he was to be the Eldest Son.

The Second Master ushered us graciously to comfortable wicker chairs on the verandah, and the maid served us tea. He told us about the birds—canaries and thrushes and others I did not recognize—hanging in cages from the beams and rafters. He told us about his flowers in pots piled high in orderly rows on a series of step-like shelves under the windows.

The little bungalow was at the very back of the garden which stretched from the back of the compound to the front wall. This then was the garden that every great house must have, the garden that was beautiful all the year around: where the evergreens grew and the shrubs that were decorative even when without leaf or bloom, the "welcome to spring" that we call forsythia, flowering almond, hibiscus, and tea roses; where the perennials, peonies, and jade hairpin blossoms that we call August lilies and chrysanthemums bloomed in their rotations. It was only three courtyards deep, but as we wandered along the winding paths between the shrubs and the raised bed for the perennials and the skillfully placed trees it seemed as if we had been walking in a much larger space, so cleverly did the paths wind through the scenery.

"This garden had been neglected before we came," the Second Master said. "There has been much to do to it and it is not yet finished." There was pride of achievement in his eyes as he led us between the overhanging weeping willows and the peony beds raised high on their carved brick platforms. "You must come again when they are in bloom." I knew that peonies were one of the main prides of a scholar's garden. Every spring I saw the men whose lives were spent over books looking at the imperial collection of peonies in one of the parks of the Forbidden City now open to the public, looking at them with admiration and almost reverence.

"We are repairing the lotus pool." The vigorous serenity of her walk matched the active serenity of her eyes as Lao Tai-tai took over the conversation. "Soon we will have water in it and lotus plants. This little bridge will be painted red." She was immensely pleased with this large toy, and we could see that she and her son shared the taste for the garden and worked on it together. "We can't walk on the bridge, it is not yet safe. Remember the workman I brought to your clinic? He fell when one of the posts gave way. The next time you come the bridge will be ready. It is difficult to get workmen who have had experience in fitting the zig-zag corners and propping them correctly." Lao Tai-tai led us around the pool to the pavilion on the south side, facing north, overlooking the pool. "See how nice and cool it is—a wonderful place to sit on a hot summer day." They did not need to go to the seashore for their summers. They had their summer resorts in their own compounds. They built for all four seasons—those who had money.

Standing in the pavilion, which was slightly raised, we could see to the east, over a broken wall being mended by a couple of workmen dressed in the traditional indigo-blue coats and trousers, over into a kitchen garden stretching toward the city wall. The Second Master saw me looking across the space and said, "We have just bought that piece of land and added it to the property. The wall was in a very bad condition. We have pulled it down and are rebuilding it." A few workmen were busy making mud bricks at the far end of the garden, and in another place a gardener was sifting the soil, preparing the special beds.

Lao Tai-tai led us then through the Eastern Moongate—opposite the Western Moongate through which we had started our tour—back into the Entrance Court. Here the Second Master bade us farewell and returned to his own quarters. Had we been led to the Great Gate, now before us, to indicate that the visit was over? Even then I should have known Lao Tai-tai better. She was saving the best for the last. She led us past the Spirit Screen toward the Second Gate, that beautiful gate, flanked by four great tall trees, at which I had looked so longingly when we had passed it on our way in.

"Not even in the Imperial Palace are there four such trees growing together. They have been growing many hundreds of years. They are of a rare species. They have two in the Imperial Palace that are older than these, but nowhere four together."

The trees were indeed fine and tall and straight. The branches made a design against the sky like those seen in old prints. The leaves were now tiny red buds.

"You must come when the tree is in bloom. It is covered with big purple trumpets."

We stood and let the "trumpet trees" lead our eyes up and out. Lao Tai-tai was giving us time to examine the Second Gate in detail. This gate was in the wall separating the Entrance Court from the Master Court and so had its own roof. The graceful swing of the roof, with its tiles laid like water rippling down its sides, hung from the raised ridge pole that ended in the conventional dragon finials. The beams were painted with scenes from Chinese mythology, red and green and gold, but the main points of pride were the corbels and brackets holding up the roof and its heavy rafters, painted red and ending in decorative tiles. The crowning glory was a pair of "hanging brackets" shaped like lotus buds and painted in realistic colors.

"Artists ask to come and see them," said Lao Tai-tai with pride, the pride of possession and also the pride in beauty.

There was no need for Lao Tai-tai to deprecate her possessions with the customary polite terms. These things were bigger and beyond her, but even in smaller things she did not trouble to be conventional. She was one who was able to be courteous either within or without the pattern.

We went through the Second Gate into a broad, almost square courtyard, the largest courtyard we had yet seen. It was fitting that it should be the largest since it was the main courtyard of the compound, the Courtyard of the Master. It was paved with brick. I could see that the flower beds under the windows had been tended and a few plants put out. There was, however, an empty feeling in the court, as if it had been swept clean of all the personality it might once have had. In small houses this was the busiest court of all, the most lived-in place. In great homes, where each branch of the family had its own courtyard and its own small kitchen (the clan kitchen was for the staple foods only in many large houses), this would still have had many signs of being lived in. I wondered if what we missed were not the Old Man's bird cages and the stools he liked to sit on and his special plants.

The house on the far side of the court was taller than any of the others in the compound, and therefore longer and deeper, because a chien is a fixed proportion between height, width, and depth and all the main houses were of five chien. That could be seen from the pillars holding up the roof, even if one did not count the windows or see into the rooms. Here again was a railless verandah running the width of the house. Like the overhang of the roof in smaller houses it was the right width to let in the sun in winter and keep it out in summer. Houses had been built that way since the dawn of history.

The two houses against the east and west walls were second-ary houses and of three chien each. One seemed to have some-one living in it; its door (there was only one to each house and that in the center) was slightly ajar. There was a chain and pad-lock on the door of the east house. It was probably used as a storeroom.

A smiling maidservant, her hair combed smoothly back from her face and into the conventional knot at the nape of her neck, dressed in the long gown of blue cotton cloth worn by the working people of the city, held up the door curtain. The stew-ard apparently had returned to his regular duties and was no-where in sight. The only other servant visible was the wet nurse carrying Little Root. They could be seen through the open door.

Little Root's mother and sister and Lao Tai-tai's daughter greeted us as we entered and were with us the rest of our visit. They sat quietly listening and watching. It was Lao Tai-tai's party and they spoke only when addressed by one of us. Some-times I thought I saw a flash in the eyes of Lao Tai-tai's daugh-ter, showing that she did not agree with her mother, but I was never sure since the heavy lids fell quickly. The set of the cheek-bones and the chin gave promise of a vigor like her mother's and her eyes and mouth showed an intelligence at work.

We had entered a large room, two chien in one. The first im-pression was of graciousness and harmony, of things being in their right places and of the right things being around. There was the faint fragrance of many things blended, jasmine flow-ers and incense, musk and sandalwood, indigo and the earth itself of which the houses were so largely made. There was as much of a lived-in feeling here as there had been a lack of it in the courtyard. Against the wooden partition on the east were four straight-backed chairs of red hardwood. The thick flat cushions on the chairs were covered with blue and white sten-ciled cloth. I had never before seen this cloth used in any home of wealth. It was the people's cloth—beautiful in its clear white and indigo blue, its designs of stylized flowers and leaves, and its homespun texture. The same cloth was on the cushions of the two seats fixed against the wall, on either side of the tea table, in the ceremonial bay at the back of the room. This, opposite the entrance door, was the place of honor where the Master received guests who must be received formally. In front of this bay was where chairs would be placed when the Honorable Old Ones sat to be honored by their descendants.

To indicate the division between the two chien of the big room a valance of carved wood hung from the cross beam. Just beyond this and toward the back was a square table of polished black wood with four black wood stools around it. This then was where Lao Tai-tai ate her meals when she was not eating them in some place of her fancy.

Against the west wall was a long ceremonial table—a wall table, very long and narrow. On it were the usual vases of artificial flowers and a piece of Yunnan stone, framed and standing. The black or grey or brown infiltrations in this marble have always suggested scenes to Chinese scholars who delight to let their imaginations play. They can look at these designs of nature's chance and see all manner of visions. These they treasured centuries before there was impressionism or non-objective art in the Western world.

In front of the long table was a smaller table. On this were placed the incense burner and plates of fruit and cakes. I looked up to see to whom they were offered. On the wall hung the large framed photograph of an old man. He had a benign face with smooth regular features and a long sparse beard. One eye was defective. I did not need to be told that the picture was of Old Mr. Yin.

We sat and drank tea and chatted. Lao Tai-tai was giving us a chance to get used to the place. She saw my eye wandering and answered many of my questions before I could ask them.

"Would you like to see my bedroom?" There was evident pride in the question.

The daughter lifted the curtain in the doorway on the east, in the wooden partition. My heart sank and stayed low for a long time. We had entered a bare room with a foreign chest of drawers, a copy of Grand Rapids's best varnished pine, and a single brass bedstead. I remembered the pleasant rooms in similar homes where the kang, the built-in brick bed stretching from wall to wall under the window, was a warm nest covered with a yellowing matting of braided kaoliang straw and piled high on either end with folded quilts of gay colors. There would be heavy red-wood chests and wardrobes against the walls, giving dignity to the room. I groaned inwardly. I could not see Lao Tai-tai living in this hard, bare, foreign room. I could not say anything but tried to make a polite murmur.

"I had a foreign bath put in also," she said, motioning toward the western part of the house, "but it is too much trouble to use. I am old-fashioned." I looked around the room that was so blatantly new, and Lao Tai-tai caught my eye and smiled. "Well, anyway, I find the old ways of keeping clean suit me. Sometimes my daughter has a hot bath in the big tub."

I still could not imagine Lao Tai-tai sleeping on the soft mattress of that brass-framed bed. I remembered how bitterly our patients from the country districts complained of the soft hospital beds and how many of them asked to be allowed to sleep on the floor—was it not covered with wood? This Western furniture did not seem to suit her—to be in harmony with her. Had she been caught by the current fashion for the "modern," as all Western things were called? Had she been caught by the newness of the forms and designs and confused newness of design with beauty? That I could not believe. The intrinsic beauty of the old Chinese furniture is such that we filled our homes with it; wherever I have seen it, in whatever kind of house, it sits serenely and at home. Perhaps it was the young daughter who had taken advantage of the changes to be made after the Old Master's death and had insisted on going modern. This was the period when "modern" was a word on everyone's lips, was a word of praise to most. It was the period, the late nineteen-twenties, when many in the old country were losing faith in their own ways of doing things. Their own age-old way of life was not bringing to them the wealth and power the Westerners now had, even though in past centuries and millennia it had brought them more than any of the little Western nations had possessed. But I could not see Lao Tai-tai confusing values. And as I looked at the daughter I felt that she also would know, would learn, to discard that which should be discarded and to keep that which was eternal in their way of life.

I barely noticed the little door in the far wall leading to the easternmost room. That was where the unmarried daughters always slept, in the room beyond their parents' room, with no outside door of its own.

When we came back into the living room the maid was coming in from the back passageway rolling a big round table top. This back passageway was found in the great houses and was on the north side, where it made an added protection against the north winds as well as a quick way to the courtyard behind. It also gave added storage space. The maid slid the round table top dextrously over onto the square table. Then she set eight pairs of chopsticks and eight little bowls with eight china spoons on its polished surface and again disappeared down the passageway. When she came back she carried a huge round platter—a foot and a half, perhaps two feet, in diameter—heaped with a gleaming mass of white in which many bits of color had been set in a pattern like a mosaic and covered with a glistening white sauce. It was the famous sweet dish of the North—the Pa Pao Fan—the confection of the Eight Precious Things.

"Come," said Lao Tai-tai as she indicated our seats. "I know all foreigners like sweets, and," turning to me, "I know you like Pa Pao Fan." Li Kuan had been talking, it was clear. "That's another place where you and I are alike. We both like sticky sweet things to eat, and this dish my maid makes well." She took up a big china spoon and began to stir the pattern—candied green plums, red fruit, dates, lotus seeds, ginko nuts, watermelon seeds, eight kinds in all—into the round of glutinous rice. She mixed it all with the hot sugar sauce flavored with rose leaves and put some into a bowl for each of us.

Then she began to laugh softly and gaily as she looked around the table and saw the four of us, all of us older than her daughter or even her daughter-in-law and yet not married, and as she thought of her tale. "Only one other woman have I ever known who liked this dish as much as we do. She was an old maid. She was forty when she married. She had been far too precious to her parents for them to let her go. They had never been able to find a man good enough for her. She married this widower with grown sons. They really liked each other." Lao Tai-tai giggled appreciatively. "They liked each other so much they amazed their children, who could not understand that such old people," her eyes twinkled, "could be in love." Lao Tai-tai was telling us indirectly that we could still have hope.

"In the evenings, when the children would go to their father's room to cheer the poor old parents, do their filial duty, they would soon be pushed out firmly, the doors brought together behind them, and the bolt slid." Lao Tai-tai's arms spread and she brought them together in the gesture we all used when we closed our double doors, a gesture that has become stylized by the actors on the stage. "The children were amazed as they stood outside the door and heard the sound of two people in merry conversation."

The party was over and it was time for us to go. We had spent an afternoon in the China of many centuries past. A door was open, however, through which the present and the future were coming.

"Come again. Come often and bring your friends with you. Bring many of your friends. You know I like a lively time."

CHAPTER 4

L ao Tai-tai came gaily into my office, alive with news. As usual she seemed not to walk on her tiny feet but to float and at the same time to give the impression of great energy and movement. She greeted me as I rose to meet her; as usual she took her seat beside my desk and as usual sat bolt upright. Again I was impressed by her ability to sit upright and not look stiff.

"Little Root has spots. It's only measles but his mother was worried." Lao Tai-tai leaned forward. She could not keep back her news. "My Fourth Son is going to marry a French woman."

I must have betrayed my surprise, a surprise with apprehension in it.

Lao Tai-tai beamed and looked subtly proud and yet somewhat worried. Part of the pride was the self-respect that is the heritage of all Chinese, part her own special distinction, and part the pride of a marriage in her family that could not be easily achieved. This last pride was tempered, however, with a feeling of disappointment that her son was mixing his life stream with that of another race—it would be better to say, of another culture. The Chinese had but recently begun to be conscious of race.

The Chinese—as do every people—have a strong conviction of their own superiority, and in their case it is based on a rich culture and history of many thousand years. Through the past centuries and millennia all foreigners—barbarians—had acknowledged the Chinese superiority. It was in this last century only that there had come "barbarians" in any number who had at their command superior force and ways to make the earth yield more of its riches and transform them into more of the things that people use. These "big crude" people had machines

47

to make more goods. They also knew more about the ways to cure diseases. Though still barbarians in many ways, they had abilities and knowledge that made up to some extent for their lack of real civilization, of graciousness in living and the art of human relations. Because the foreigners had power and wealth, to be able to marry one of their women had become to some Chinese a badge of having arrived in this new world where the Westerner was dominant. It showed also that the family had money enough to afford the luxury of one of these women who spent so much money and needed so many more things than a Chinese woman. Yet to most it was still an outrage. All these things I saw in Lao Tai-tai's face. Then she smiled, and the smile and the little gesture she made as she settled back very slightly in her seat said clearly, "Not every student in France can come back with a French wife." It was a feat, but it was also a problem, and she was going to put the very best face she could on it.

She smiled again as she saw me wipe away the look of concern that had started to show on my face and try to make it blank. "They say that if a Chinese is to marry a foreign woman it is best to marry a French woman."

Lao Tai-tai's friends, it was clear, had been trying to comfort her and help her put the best face on a development that none of them liked but none could control. Also she was asking me to say my words of assurance—if I could.

"They say," she went on, "that French women are the best cooks among foreigners."

"None can compare with Chinese," I said politely and truthfully.

"Also," said Lao Tai-tai, "they are the most careful in spending. They are not as careless about money or as wasteful as the women of other foreign countries—not as great spenders." Then suddenly realizing that she was speaking to one of these others—a realization that rarely came into our conversations—she said, "Of course you are more like a Chinese."

I smiled, and the faint barrier Lao Tai-tai felt she had put up was blown away like a gossamer.

48

"They can make their own clothes, too, I am told. Still, a French daughter-in-law will be more expensive than a Chinese daughter-in-law."

I hastened to be as reassuring as I could. But I thought of the long succession of mixed marriages I had seen, and hoped, for the sake of my friend and for all in the family, that the girl the Fourth Master was marrying was one who had the vision and the humanity to act like a Chinese wife since she was marrying a Chinese and returning to live in China. The burden of making a mixed marriage a success, as I had seen, was always on the wife. The better her understanding and her heart, the better the chance of happiness for the young couple and for the family. If she was one who could see only the way things were done in her own circle and in her own land, the only hope of any constructive life and happiness would be for the couple to return to France.

Lao Tai-tai smiled the direct and heartwarming smile that made us all love her, the smile that said, "No matter what comes, life is grand and each new thing that comes is something to meet, to deal with, to savor, and to enjoy." Again I wondered from what kind of family Lao Tai-tai had come and what kind of life she had led that she had this capacity to so great a degree.

After Lao Tai-tai had left, Li Kuan, who had come into the room to greet her, said, "She is not as happy about the marriage as she tries to make out." Li Kuan called often at the house to see Little Root and picked up the family gossip. "She has been looking for a wife for the Fourth Master, so he could marry as soon as he got back from France. She had picked out a Peking girl of good family, well educated and—this time—a pretty one."

I knew that Li Kuan's "this time" referred to the Second Master's marriage to the well-educated daughter of a good family who now looked out on life with the patient expression of the lonely woman who has never been pretty.

"Lao Tai-tai wrote him about the girl and said she would wait until he got back to conclude the contract with the girl's family. She wanted him first to see the girl. The news of his planned marriage to the French woman was the answer to her letter."

It had been a great concession to the modernism of the young for Lao Tai-tai to offer to let him see the girl before she, as head of the family, made the contract with the other family. It was very modern of her. The brutal abruptness of his reply was also modern and very young. But how was he to know that his mother had youthful eyes and that no brutality was needed where the chains of the past bound so lightly? And I wondered again what had tempered her natural understanding that she should be able to hold on to the good in the old and see the good in the new and not be confused.

"How does the other family take it?" I asked Li Kuan.

"The contract had not been signed, so there were no real grounds for making trouble. But to ask them to wait was hard on the family when they were told the matter was all off. They lost a certain amount of face."

"And hard on Lao Tai-tai."

"But that is not the only trouble Lao Tai-tai has now—though this other is lesser and constantly with them."

"Is there something wrong with the Second Master's family?" I said before thinking that Li Kuan's statement did not exactly fit.

"Oh no. The baby was born all right—a beautiful, a very beautiful boy. And she is pregnant again." That would be the young concubine. "There will be a year only between the children. No—it's the Third Master. He has again lost his job and come home. And because the Second Master has a concubine he thinks he must have one too. She also is from a "House with Wide Gates" but not a young one such as the Second Master married—one who was still a virgin. This one had been receiving guests for several years. I do not like her. She is stupid. I think there will be trouble."

"Perhaps," I said, "she will join the other two—her husband and the wife—and all three keep themselves sodden in opium and have no energy for making trouble."

50

Li Kuan pushed that aside. "The Second Master will be trying to get him another job now."

"What kind?"

"He's not good for much—a secretary at the barracks, probably. He has lost so many jobs in Tientsin that the Second Master's connections in the yamen, among the officials, have almost all been used up."

I nodded and returned to my heaped-up desk, wondering again at the strength and love of life that could make my old friend see the joy there was in life when there was so much trouble.

CHAPTER 5

I was having breakfast in my courtyard, enjoying the early autumn sunshine, the air with its welcome crispness, and the blue sky. I too liked to have my meals where the fancy took me, but my possibilities were more limited than Lao Tai-tai's. The cook—who doubled as "boy" (steward and general manager) in this little house—had placed a rattan chair and a tea table in the corner of the court where I would get the sunshine and see the row of pine trees, green against the blue sky, and the roof line of the East House where it met the wall. There was nothing more serious on my mind than thinking idly that the lattice-work of the dining room and living room windows (and this meant the whole front of both the little adobe houses) would be better for a coat of paint, and wondering what I would wear to the dance that night.

The cook poured my second cup of coffee. I had never been able to get him to leave the coffee pot on the table. He seemed to feel that would lessen his dignity. Also his professional pride was involved in having it always hotter than I could drink. "Yin Lao Tai-tai has sent a motor-car for you. She wants you to go to her. She's at the hospital."

Something in his voice made me ask, "How long has the car been here?"

"Lao Tai-tai said you were not to be told until you had finished your breakfast."

The trouble then could not be too serious. But as I walked down the path to the gate, and as the car trundled through the hutungs, out to Hatamen Street, and to the hospital, I was wondering what could have happened to Little Root or his sister, or to Lao Tai-tai herself.

The car turned in through the iron gates of the hospital and around the marble approach to the accident ward. There was no one sitting on the benches against the corridor walls. I asked the white-clad figure hurrying by where Lao Tai-tai was.

"Oh, we asked her to sit in one of the examining rooms. It is a little more comfortable," and she waved me toward one.

My soft-soled shoes made no sound as I walked into the room. Never before had I seen Lao Tai-tai look tired. She sat on the chair—on the edge as always—almost straight. There was a slight sag to her shoulders, but the weariness was not of the body, it was of the soul.

"The trouble?" I said.

She sprang up and came toward me. I clasped her hands. Whatever it was, she had sent for me as a friend and needed comforting.

"It's the Third Daughter-in-law, the Secondary one." Even behind their backs Lao Tai-tai gave face to her concubine daughters-in-law and called them by their honorary title—the Secondary Daughter-in-law, a euphemistic way of saying concubine.

"Oh," I said, puzzled that the illness of one whom I knew Lao Tai-tai did not like and considered unnecessary should so trouble her.

"She tried to kill herself. She drank opium."

I drew Lao Tai-tai back to the chairs. This was serious. Loved or not, a suicide was serious. One did not want death for any-one, and that of a daughter-in-law could mean trouble for the whole family. I remembered the suicides of daughters-in-law I had heard of in my childhood and those who had been brought to the hospital after drinking water in which matches had been soaked or "stealing opium" from their fathers-in-law. There were those about whom we heard, who had jumped down wells when nothing else was available. Everyone would say, "Her destiny was not a good one," but the destiny of which they spoke was not that she had had to commit suicide but that she had been driven to suicide by her wrongs, which usually meant a cruel mother-in-law. I knew that was not the cause of this young woman's attempt. The Third Master and his wives lived away from home most of the time, in Tientsin. Even when at home they had their own courtyard and their own house of five chien. This gave each of the wives a room of her own, one on either side of the living room. They could live for days on end and never see other members of the larger family. Their maidservant would bring them their food, cooked in the main family kitchen. They could go out of the compound and come back to their own house through the Bamboo Pavilion Courtyard and never go near the courtyards where the others lived. Lao Tai-tai, we knew, did not interfere with them, with the way they lived. What had made the young concubine try to commit suicide could not have been the usual story, but the results to the family could be as serious. If she died it would mean lawsuits and much money to her family, if she had a family. Even if she had no family there could be those who would claim, under the circumstances, to be her family, and there would be much trouble. "The Yin Family has driven our daughter to suicide." That would be the complaint even if those who complained were the ones who had sold her originally to the House with the Wide Gates.

There was something more, however, in Lao Tai-tai's face. It was not only concern for the Family, though that was there in great measure.

"She is such a silly little thing," and it was clear that Lao Tai-tai did not like silliness, "but still she is a human being, and it is not easy to be a concubine." But there was more. "My Third Son—he is silly, too."

I had never heard her talk about her Third Son. I had never met him. She talked often about the Fourth—with pride and with the love for the youngest. And there was always the sense of the Second being with her. He was her partner in all their affairs. She counted on him.

She did not seem to see the case of instruments and bottles and the oxygen tanks around us that so fascinated most people when they were in these little rooms. She saw only—this once at least—what was on her mind. "They quarreled last night. Something of no consequence. The three of them quarreled and he sided with the Wife. So 'she' (the concubine) took opium. Fortunately my son got up in the middle of the night. Those who smoke opium have no regularity of life. When he woke from his opium he heard her breathing in a strange way. He called us and we brought her here. The doctors say she did not take too large a dose and they think they can save her."

I let Lao Tai-tai talk. That was one of the reasons for my being there.

"Ai," she said, "my Third is so silly. The Second took a concubine so he must take one. The Second adopted a son so he must adopt a child also. They have taken a little girl—an eight-year-old little girl. I think she is their amah's (maidservant's) daughter. Perhaps the amah talked them into it. Always he is copying his brother and not doing it as well."

Lao Tai-tai sighed. "This is not the first time the silly little thing has tried to kill herself. In Tientsin she jumped out of an upstairs window and broke her leg. How much trouble that was to all of us! It is very difficult to die jumping out of so low a window."

"Perhaps she doesn't really want to die."

"No, she does not really want to die. She wants to make us trouble. She is no more unhappy now than she has always been. She's a silly little thing. She does not have the eyes in her heart and mind that would make her a person of understanding, or of consequence. Nor has my son. Come, let us go and see her, and ask the nurse to take good care of her. Will you talk to the doctor and ask him in detail about her?" This was my official reason for being called—that I might be the official friend at court.

Together we walked through the long corridors to the private patients' pavilion, to the floor of the semiprivate rooms. Lao Tai-tai had taken the young woman at her own evaluation, or perhaps the funds to pay for her stay in the hospital would come from the earnings of the Third himself and not from the Family.

Two white-clad nurses were walking a figure dressed in the shapeless light-blue hospital robe, one on each side grasping her arms firmly. Up and down the corridor they shuffled past us, forcing her to move—much against her drugged will. The face, bloated from opium, might under usual circumstances be pert and pretty.

In the background I saw a tall, weedy young man. He came toward us. "My Third Son," Lao Tai-tai murmured. The tall thin figure stooped. It was not the cultivated stoop of the scholar. It was the stoop of weakness—physical and of the spirit. As I looked at him I felt that he had never in his life done anything he knew to be acceptable. It must have been difficult to have been brought up with an older brother who was so able and must always have been so able. How could Lao Tai-tai have borne such a son as this? He did not look like her. He did not look like his Second Brother. I had never seen the other two. He did not look like either of his sisters: neither the young one who looked so much like Lao Tai-tai nor the older one, Lao Tai-tai's eldest child, whom I had seen briefly during one of my visits to the house. She was a middle-aged woman with a hard square face it was difficult to believe had ever been pretty or attractive. She looked like the wife of a country shopkeeper without the dignity of the land behind her or of the world before her. This son, the Third, faintly suggested an elongated and blurred copy of what the Old Man, whose picture hung on Lao Tai-tai's wall, might have looked like when he was young.

I murmured a few words to the young man and went off in search of the doctor. He would tell me, I knew, exactly what he had told Lao Tai-tai and her son, but it would comfort them to have it come from me also, from one who was their friend and who was also of the hospital staff.

CHAPTER 6

Several months later Lao Tai-tai came to tea at my home. It was one of the beautiful sunny days so common in Peking but never treated by us with the neglect of something seen often. Each new golden day was a miracle. But it was winter. There was ice in the shade under the trees, and I had a fire in the fireplace as well as in the little pot-bellied stove.

I had invited several of my American friends to meet Lao Tai-tai. We sat around my living room and chatted. Lao Tai-tai was the gayest of all. She told us how fast Little Root was growing, how intelligent and strong he was. "You should see his feet. They are this wide," and laughingly she measured between her hands a width impossible for any human foot.

We began to talk of portents and visions. "Once I saw a rain dragon," Lao Tai-tai said. I gasped inwardly. I hoped my gasp had not been evident to the guests. Lao Tai-tai had accepted us fully, trusted me and my friends. Frank and outgoing as she was and secure within herself, she would not have talked so freely to most foreigners. There was always the chance they would laugh, and to be laughed at was something no Chinese could take lightly. They well knew the difference between being laughed at and being laughed with. "It was midsummer," she went on, "during the rainy season. It had been raining for many days. The sky was thick with clouds, broken and heavy. I saw the great dragon working his way up the clouds. His huge long body stretched from earth to heaven and was heavy as though full of water. He was weaving from side to side as he worked his way up to the sky and pushed himself up out of sight."

This was an auspicious portent. The dragon was an imperial creature who controlled the life-giving waters—the rain and the rivers. Only those whose destinies were strong could have borne such a vision, and only to the strong and fortunate did such visions come—portents of good. Lao Tai-tai was one to whom fortune came and one strong enough to bear it when it came.

"My husband said that if I had seen a dragon, he at least had once met spirits from the Kingdom of Yuan Wang (the Prince of the Underworld)—the spirits of those who help people kill themselves."

As I translated her story to my other guests I explained that the soul of anyone who had committed suicide is bound to the place of his deed until his ghost is able to persuade someone else to take his place by committing suicide in turn at that spot and so continue the vigil. People hurry by roadside wells, cliffs, and trees with low branches. Those are places where these ghosts and their underworld helpers, the messengers of Yuan Wang, linger. One should not give them a chance to put notions into one's head. If the Old Lord had met the messengers from Yuan Wang, he had been in great danger.

"It was when he was a boy—about thirteen. From the time he was seven until he was seventeen he was with the Taiping Army." This was the army of the great revolt, in the middle of the nineteenth century, against the Manchu Dynasty, the great effort to enter the modern world and be free of the old, and particularly of the Manchu Dynasty. By all the laws of history that dynasty had been ready then to pass away as had so many dynasties before it when their days were over. "He was a beautiful and well-grown boy, so he was adopted by one of the Taiping princes, one close to the Heavenly King himself, and was called the Little Prince. He wore dragon shoes and the dragon robe.

"There was fighting most of those years. As they fought they 'went from place to place, conquering as they went.' In each place the best house was given to the prince leading the army and was called the Imperial Palace. In Soochow the house they used was exceptionally grand. And the grandest apartment, deep in the courtyards, was chosen by the soldiers for the young prince. The fighting was over and it was late at night, so they took him into a room, set the guard, and told him to go to sleep.

"It was a woman's room, probably the room of one of the unmarried daughters of the house. There were huge beams of polished wood. The hanging of the bed and the covers of the quilts were of brocaded silk. There was a fragrance of perfumes in the air. Three big bronze braziers of burning charcoal warmed the room. Candles of red wax, a foot tall, in high hardwood stands, still lighted the room. The people who lived in the house must have just left."

Lao Tai-tai was enjoying the sixty-year-old story as much as we.

"The little boy lay down on the soft quilts on the bed but he could not sleep. He was frightened and he did not know why he was frightened. He had followed the army for six years and should not have been frightened of anything: but he was frightened.

"As the boy lay there the bed began to shake. It shook as though some being of great strength was angry that he should be in the bed and was trying to shake him out. The light in the braziers blazed up and died down, and the candles guttered almost to extinction and then lit up again. This they did three times, and the bed continued to shake.

"At last in his fright he managed to scream. The guards rushed in to save their prince. They searched the room. They found, behind the curtain that separated the bed from the wall, a beautiful young woman hanging by her sash from a beam. She was dead, but her body was still warm.

"Of what this was a portent we have never been sure. It showed, however, the strength of his destiny. The suicide demons could not hurt him. The grave of his mother was in a place auspicious for the fortunes of the descendants, and its influence was strong enough to overcome the strength of the ghosts."

I wanted to ask where the mother was buried. It was evident there was a story. Grave sites were chosen with as much care as the family resources allowed because of their influence over future generations of the family. I wanted to know how the Old Master came to be with the Taiping Army, and more of what happened to him. Not every boy who lived with the army became a prince. But the conversation went forward too fast. Lao Tai-tai was in the midst of another story.

"Grave sites can have no lasting effects for good to the family unless the sons and daughters are filial. Heaven hates an unfilial son. Those who do not honor their parents are struck with thunder. I have seen it myself. There was a young man in the village where I was brought up who was lazy and would not work. His mother scolded him and he reviled her. He said words to her that no son should say to his mother. The gods sent the thunder to strike him. There was a great crash. The thunder struck him on the leg. It rolled along the beam in a fiery ball to the house of the neighbors and burned their room. The young man's leg shriveled, and he was lame ever afterwards. There was a scorched place in the beam to show where the thunderball rolled, and there was the burnt house next door."

Lao Tai-tai finished the story with spirit but did not seem comfortable. Even while talking she had been looking around. She had barely finished when she stood up. "I'd like to walk in the courtyard."

I went out with her.

"The fire—it's too warm for me."

Her seat, as fitting for the guest of honor, had been opposite the door—the most honorable position in the room—but it was also the one next to the fireplace.

"You see," she said, "my clothes are padded with silk waste and are very warm. See how thick," and she lifted the corner of her knee-length grey silk coat for me to feel. "I do not have a fire in my house unless it is very cold. I like to be able to go outdoors and indoors as I please. I do not like to put on more clothes when I go out and take them off when I come in: changing every time I turn around. And I work in the garden. There is so much to do in the garden, even in winter."

I sympathized. Although I did not dress as warmly as Lao Tai-tai, I suffered in the homes of my friends and often felt stifled with the heat. I am afraid they often felt cold in mine.

"Now I'm all right," said Lao Tai-tai. "I'm going to sit next to the door."

So, her gay self again, she returned to the living room and I placed her chair next to the open door. Comfortable and relaxed, she looked around the room and giggled, if the sound she made could be called a giggle—so full was it of dignity, the knowledge of people and of their ways in the world, and an acceptance of their ways and of them as people. Also it was full of gaiety.

She was looking around the room at the circle of Western women sitting as Western women sit, with their knees crossed and their feet stretched out before them. The feet were ordinary American feet—not unduly large, but immense when compared to Lao Tai-tai's or even to those of her daughter, which had never been bound.

"There isn't one of you," said Lao Tai-tai, "who has feet as large as those of my French daughter-in-law."

There was a catch in my breath. Things could not be going as well with the family and the French daughter-in-law as Lao Tai-tai had hoped. I wondered what was the trouble and knew that in time I would know. To say that her daughter-in-law's feet were big was to criticize her. The size of a woman's feet in old China was something the women and especially their mothers, and so their families, could control. A pretty face was given by Heaven, and no family could be blamed if their daughter did not have one. To criticize her feet was to indicate that something else was wrong, something she could have controlled. Also to compare her feet with ours was to say that what was wrong was something Western about her and at the same time to hope that she would be Western in the way we were Western, that in time she would perhaps understand the ways of her new family and accept them as we did.

Then I thought of the story of the unfilial son. That Lao Tai-tai should have followed that line of thought rather than any one of the others opened out by her story made me realize that lack of filial piety, of consideration for the Elders in the Family, must have been on her mind this day.

Later, Li Kuan told me about the homecoming of the bride. In the old Chinese pattern, thousands of years old, in the pattern of society where people lived by tilling the soil and things were made by hand, engagements were contracts between families. The wedding was the bringing home of the bride to the man's family, the announcement to the world that she was now a member of this other family. Drums and gongs were beaten and banners flown to announce to the world that the girl in the embroidered red chair was being taken to her new home. In the new home the groom knelt with his bride before the ancestors—both those who lived on the other side of the invisible barrier, whose tablets were set in a row on the long table against the north wall, and those on this side of the barrier, who were seated in red decorated chairs—and also to other relatives higher in family rank than he. That was when the woman was accepted into the family. This was part of the old agricultural-handicraft pattern of life where families lived in the villages among their neighbors and took their brides from nearby villages. Even as the new pattern began to develop and men to range abroad—not only as officials, but where the new ways of trade and mechanized industry took them—and to marry as it suited them personally, still the pattern of courtesy and honor to the family persisted. I thought of my friend from Albany who had married one of the Chinese doctors. She lived in a Chinese compound and house, as Chinese as any other in the city on the outside and as Albany on the inside as the furniture and books and pictures brought across the ocean from America could make it. The life she and her Chinese husband led in that house was lived on Western lines, for the doctor had been educated abroad and liked Western food and Western ways. It was said, however, that when he took her as a bride to the old home village, to meet his mother and the relatives, she got down on her knees and made the correct obeisance to those higher in family rank than she. All the family and friends held her in honor.

When the Fourth brought his wife home from Paris, where he had married her according to alien ways, the family would, according to custom, make a ceremony of the homecoming. Not only would the steward be waiting at the gate to welcome them, there would be red silk scarves hanging on the gate to show a "happy occasion" was in progress, a bride expected, and the steward would be flanked by a corps of the lesser relatives. They would not conduct the bride and groom to the library to which we had been taken, but to the center of the home, to Lao Tai-tai's room. She was the highest generation on this side of the invisible curtain. She would be sitting alone in the place of honor opposite the door. Perhaps there would be a chair beside hers on which would be placed the photograph of the Old Master. On her left—the next place of honor—would be the Second Son and his Wife, if the First Son had not come from the country for the occasion, and on her right would be the Third and his Wife. They would all be dressed in their ceremonial robes, the men in their long blue silk gowns and short black satin topcoats, the formal dress of the Republic; and the women in red embroidered skirts and black embroidered satin coats that came to their knees. The concubines in their green satin skirts with their black embroidered satin coats, like those of the wives, and the children in all their gay clothes, would be standing in the west room, where we had sat around the table and eaten the Eight Precious Things confection when we had visited Lao Tai-tai. The servants would place mats on the ground in front of the Second, and then in front of the Third. In turn the couple would be expected to kneel and make the obeisance to each in turn and be welcomed into the family.

Perhaps the family would act in a modern way and not dress in all the formal robes or insist on all the ceremonial. Still they would expect the bride and groom to kneel before the ancestors and before Lao Tai-tai.

Li Kuan told me what happened.

"I visited the Yin Family today." She was fond of the family and welcome whenever she went.

"How is Little Root?"

"He's fine."

I wondered why she did not go into details about him as she usually did.

"How is Lao Tai-tai?"

"She's fine. But she's not happy. No one there is very happy these days. The French daughter-in-law won't eat Chinese food and she won't cook for herself. They have to hire a cook who knows foreign ways just for her—a lot of extra expense. She won't do a thing for herself, and she complains all the time to the Fourth Master. She can't speak Chinese and she won't try to learn. She wants the Fourth Master to stay with her all the time and interpret for her."

This was trouble indeed. This was not a woman adjusting to her husband's family. This was not a woman of understanding with a generous heart. Perhaps it was a frightened woman: certainly it was a selfish one. It is not easy for a woman to be away from the land where she was born and brought up, away from her own family and friends, and to live in a land that was strange, but she had married a man of that strange land.

And then Li Kuan's face had become stern. "She even refused to kneel to Lao Tai-tai when the Fourth brought her home."

In my mind's eye I could see her standing—stiff and awkward and strange, like a stick of wood in the midst of gracious, dignified human beings.

She had committed the greatest wrong of all. If there was resentment and anger in her heart, there was wrath and a deep sense of utter outrage in theirs.

Li Kuan stood silent a minute as she was leaving and then said, "She is very beautiful in the foreign fashion—the French wife of the Fourth. She was one of those who walk around in shops showing off clothes."

64

CHAPTER 7

Lao Tai-tai had long since persuaded the secretary in my outer office that she need not be announced. She came in as she pleased, and I was always glad to see her. I rose and greeted her as she walked quickly across the room.

She smiled, settled herself on the edge of the chair, and said, "Buying milk powder for Little Root. What a lot he uses! He is growing so fast." Then her face clouded. The change in the smooth ageless face was very slight, but I knew her well enough to see the cloud. "I want to ask your advice."

Inside my heart I sighed. I knew it must be serious, for seldom did Lao Tai-tai need advice from anyone. She knew the pattern of life and the principles on which the pattern was formed. She had had a lifetime of experience in dealing with people within that pattern of well-worked-out human relationships. All problems that came within the scope of her life were those of human relationships. To her all problems were those of human relations.

"It is the Fourth Daughter-in-law."

I had guessed as much. Even if she needed advice, it would not be to me she would come except for advice concerning the daughter-in-law from another culture, one that was near to my own. The Fourth Daughter-in-law brought in a set of values new to the pattern that had been building for many thousands of years and in which many millions of people lived. To Lao Tai-tai the principles on which her pattern was built were eternal, but she was intelligent enough, experienced enough, and secure enough within herself to know that sometimes principles were worked out in detail differently in different places.

"She wants to go home to see her mother."

I nodded. It was to be expected that she would want to return to Paris. Whether it was to see her mother or not, it was in such terms that Lao Tai-tai would think and speak of her desire to go to France.

Lao Tai-tai looked anxiously at me. "Is it necessary, according to your way of living, for the bride to go home to see her mother at stated intervals? We want to do the right thing. You know that in our way of life the bride must go to see her mother on the third day, and then from time to time at longer and longer intervals—until she gets used to her new family and as long as her mother lives. But we do not marry so far from home. We marry people in the next village or in the same city. Sometimes we marry people from other provinces and then the rules for home-going are very different. No one expects the bride to go home so often, sometimes not at all. It took many many days and much money to bring my Fourth Daughter-in-law here. They've been here only a few months. Will she want to take that long and expensive journey every year? As a woman of our Family she should think from the point of view of our Family. She should think of these things—of the expense for us. How can we send her back to her mother after only six months?"

My heart ached for my old friend.

"She says she is homesick. Any bride is homesick until she knows the new family. But she refuses to make friends with any of us. She will not learn to speak our language. She wants my son to spend all his time with her and her French friends.

"Yes, she is careful in spending, but not to help the Family. It is so she may buy more clothes and jewels for herself.

"She won't eat our food. She says we are dirty."

I winced. I was enough Chinese to feel the insult of the unfair accusation. Chinese are as meticulous about some things as Westerners are about others.

"Well," I said, trying to comfort her, "your son likes French food, I am sure, since he was so many years in the country. What she cooks for herself will suit him."

"She will do no cooking. She insists that we hire a French-trained cook."

66

"That must make trouble in your kitchen."

"Oh, she does not live with us anymore. She says she cannot live in a Chinese house."

The beauty of the spacious home floated before my eyes. She was one of the Westerners who had eyes but could not see.

"She will not live in Peking."

Whether a person loved Peking or not was for me an easy and, I had found, a true gauge of that person's quality. Peking did not yield her secrets easily. There was always something, however, that could charm one immediately, and every effort to know the city was rewarded with further knowledge of its planned beauty, of its history, of its people.

"They have a house in the French concession in Tientsin."

The barren crags of the pseudo-European city rose before my eyes.

"She can then entertain your son's friends in the French manner. That would be useful to him in his law practice: give them something different."

"She will not meet my son's friends. She will meet French people only. My son has to entertain his Chinese friends in the restaurants." She paused a moment. "He has taken a position in the university. He teaches law and French literature. He does what law practice he can on the side. It takes much money to support his home."

I did not know what were the financial arrangements between the brothers and never asked. That there was some arrangement was to be expected. I would judge from my knowledge of other families that only when in the old home would any member of the family live on family funds. In the Yin Family the Eldest Son lived on the estate in Anhwei Province—the Old Man's home province, and probably the estate he had left. Perhaps any member of the Family could go there and live as long as he liked but no money would be sent out. I had been told the estate was not large. The real money of the Family had been made by the Second. He controlled these funds—he and his mother—and the Peking home, the real Family Home. Any member living outside the Home had to support himself except for educational expenses or unusual expenses such as this journey to France, and these became family matters, matters for family decision.

My old friend leaned forward. There was deeper trouble in her eyes, trouble too deep to be caused by the things she had told me. "They quarrel," she said. "They quarrel very often. They say terrible words to each other, words that should not be said between people, by one human being to another, words that break through and wreck." She paused, "Then it is as though nothing had happened and they are good friends again."

My old friend looked at me, and in her eyes I could see the question she would not put into words, "How could one have so little self-respect as to say such things and allow such things to be said to one?" A broken surface is not easily mended: in human relations as well as in fine fabrics, in lacquer, and in china. The rarer the stuff of the surface and of that under the surface and deep within, the deeper the scar. She sensed a different standard, a different set of values, and was groping to understand. That in this last indictment her son was as much involved as the foreign woman made the pain even greater and greater also the need to understand.

How very much my old friend had to try to understand and to forgive.

CHAPTER 8

I t was eight months before I saw Lao Tai-tai again. I had been to America and back. She came to inspect my new house as soon as I told her about it, and she brought two tiny bowls of translucent Ming Dynasty porcelain, for no one may call on friends for the first time in a new house with empty hands.

Workmen were putting in the Western plumbing I was having installed for the kitchen and bathrooms. I was not allowing them to alter the shape or form of any structure. Other workmen were papering and whitewashing. I was having all the walls whitewashed in the Chinese style, for it was a Chinese house. White paper was being pasted on the ceiling made of reed lattice-work and on the wooden lattice windows across the fronts of all the houses. White paper would keep out the cold and let in the sunshine better than glass, though I had a little pane of glass set into the center of the lower half of each window so we could see out if we desired. Each little pane had its little roll of white paper for a shade, held in place with crossed red cords.

Lao Tai-tai approved of my new house—this little compound of Entrance Court and Main Court and the houses around them, the little side court for the servants and the big empty garden behind. It had been the home of a Chinese family and was now to be mine. One's house is very important. It is the third and outermost of the shells that encase us. We do not choose our bodies, but we care for them and adorn them. We choose our clothes and our houses with regard for their fitness. My house, though many times smaller than Lao Tai-tai's, was as traditional in its layout, as well-built, and as harmonious in all its levels of roofs, its proportions in the houses and courtyards, and its details.

The Entrance Court had a special feature of its own. In addition to the row of five chien across the south side there was a small building of two chien at the west end of the court instead of the usual blank wall. It could have been the Master's study or library in a small compound like this.

Lao Tai-tai looked at the little house. She looked through the Second Gate into the Main Courtyard. She could see part of the Main House and the West House. From them she could tell what other houses there were and was sure they were enough for my needs. Looking again at the little house in the Entrance Court, she said, "That would be a good place for my Fourth Son to have his law office. I would like to rent it from you."

I murmured something about its not being large enough for his use and that I had planned to make it into my kitchen. The servant's courtyard was just behind it. And while I spoke I wondered if the Fourth and his wife were trying again to live in Peking or if Lao Tai-tai was trying to lure them back to the old home.

"A kitchen should not be in the Entrance Court. You can use the kitchen the family used that was here before."

I thought of the dark two-chien room in the alleyway from the Main Courtyard to the back garden. It was as large as this house but got no sunshine and very little air. It had been the kitchen and the maid's room but I was making it into a storeroom, the only thing for which it was fit and not too fit at that, so damp and dark it was. I explained to Lao Tai-tai that I was locking the door from the little house that opened into the Entrance Courtyard and making a new one into the Servants' Courtyard.

"Perhaps," I said, "he might like these rooms." I indicated the South House, which I was turning into a guest house, with bedroom, study, and bath. Since it faced north and backed on the street it was not desirable for steady living. It had probably been used as an office by the original owner and as a place to receive guests who might not pass the Second Gate.

Whether Lao Tai-tai had noted my lack of responsiveness and her quick wit had told her what I had left unsaid, or whether she had turned the room down in her own mind when she saw the doors I had had broken through the adobe walls—the one into the Servants' Court and one into the West House of the Main Courtyard—I never knew. Perhaps she talked it over with Li Kuan, who knew something of our Western ways. But she said nothing more about renting the little house.

Several weeks later I said to Li Kuan, "Have you seen Lao Tai-tai lately?" I wanted to find out what was in the mind of my old friend before I moved into my new house and before I invited anyone to live in my guest house. I wished no embarrassment. Perhaps I could plant something in Li Kuan's mind that would help dissuade Lao Tai-tai, turn her mind from wanting to rent my little West House.

"No, it's been several weeks since I was there, but the man-servant came for Little Root's milk powder yesterday." It was quite unusual for a servant to come instead of Lao Tai-tai. "She has gone to Tientsin, he said, to help the Fourth Master set up a new office."

I could not help feeling relief. Even in the outer court it would have been difficult to have had someone coming and going who was not of my own family. I could not have refused Lao Tai-tai if she had wanted the South House.

But on this day when she looked over my house she said no more about renting any part of it for her son.

She liked my Second Gate. Though not grand like hers, it was good, and led into a courtyard of perfect proportions. An open gallery ran around the courtyard, connecting the three houses. One could walk from house to house without getting into the rain or the sunshine when it was too hot. Lao Tai-tai stood on the brick paved walk looking at the two big lilac bushes flanking the Second Gate on the inside, at the row of tall slender pine trees, like a row of pagodas at the east side of the court, at the crabapple tree, over ten feet tall, its branches growing tightly upward as though trained, which stood beside the steps into the Main House. "You'll need another crabapple to replace the one that has gone," she said, pointing to the bricked circle where the mate had stood on the other side of the low shallow steps leading to the Main House.

She paused on the verandah of the Main House and looked back at the tops of the trees, the two locust trees spreading their branches over the whole of the Entrance Court, turning it into a cave of green light. The mass of deep green above the wall framed the Second Gate. She looked long and seriously as she turned something over in her mind. "I'm afraid," she said, "that the tops of those trees are too high and thick and that you'll have to cut them back. I'm afraid they'll block the good influences from the south."

How could I tell her that not for anything would I touch a tiny twig of those trees? I loved their opulent masses of shining green leaves. Standing sturdily, one on each side of the Second Gate, they had been the first beauty I had seen as I walked into the green cavern of the Entrance Court, shaded tent-like by those branches. They had been the first things to show me this was the house I wanted. But neither did I want to hurt the feelings of the good friend who was thinking for me and trying to help me to a home where I could live in peace and prosperity. Nor did I want an argument with her. The rule that big trees must not be allowed to shade the front of any house was a good one. Sunshine brought health and well-being. If the wise men of old, who saw that sunshine in the house was good, chose to say the goodness was because of the spirits from the south (for every house, of course, faced south), what did it matter? Or if they had not connected the benefits that came from facing the houses south with the sunshine and really thought they came from the good spirits, what did it matter? Those who faced their houses south kept alive longer. These rules had been worked out long before the age of science. Man has always explained what he saw around him with what knowledge he had at the time and systemized his explanations. How often does the human race delude itself, seeming to prefer to do the right thing for any but the real reasons? Often it does the wrong thing for what are thought to be good reasons. Someday it will grow up and face facts as facts. The main houses in any compound all faced south, and the houses facing east and west were secondary. There should be no houses facing north in which people lived. My trees, however, were a wide court away from the Main House and cut off not one tiny ray of sunshine, nor were they near enough to cut off the breezes.

"Let me call a geomancer, a Master of Wind and Water," Lao Tai-tai said from the depths of her concern. She saw my face set before I had time to turn away so as not to hurt her. She walked down again into the courtyard and looked again at the roof and at the trees. "I was wrong," she said when she again joined me on the verandah. "The trees are not higher than the ridge pole of the Main House after all. I have now looked carefully and see that they do not cut off the good influences from the south."

But the next matter was not as simple. We entered the Main House. I had taken down the eight carved-wood doors swinging on their wooden pivots that separated the eastern from the central chien and had stored them, both because they were beautiful and because there might come a day when I would want to put them back up again. The three stately chien were opened into one large room. The carved wood valance on the west and the latticed frame for the doors that had been taken down on the east hung from the beams, indicating the places for the partitions. Lao Tai-tai looked around the room and pointing with her chin to the eastern chien said, "This of course is your room, where you will sleep. You had better put the partition back so you will have some privacy." It was the room in my house that corresponded to the one in hers where she slept.

"But I'm planning to leave the three chien open and have one big living room. That's to be the library end."

"Um—that's all right. You can still have your bed there." She looked at the moveable wooden kang I had placed under the window for a daybed, but I could see she did not like the plan and thought me strange at least. "It would be bad luck for you to sleep in one of the Ear Houses." These were the small houses, tacked one on either end of the Main House. Because they were

73

each a chien and had the proportions of a chien, small as they were no one felt cramped in them. "They are for the daughters and the old people."

"I'm thinking of turning the East House into my personal living quarters, with a bedroom on one side of the Entrance Chien and a study on the other."

Lao Tai-tai's face clouded. "That's the least of the three houses." She was speaking of the Main Courtyard. "It's bad luck for the Head of the House to sleep anywhere except in the chien east of the Central Chien of the Main House. The dominant force should be in the northeast corner of the house. I have made some study of the forces of Wind and Water." She added, "That house is for your Second Son and daughter-in-law, for the younger ones of the next generation." Then she smiled, knowing that I had no son and daughter-in-law, and also that having done the best she could for the well-being of her friend, she need not press the matter further. "It's a pity," she said, closing the subject, "to expose oneself to malign influences that can be avoided." Hanging in the air between us was the thought, "Perhaps these foreigners have ways of warding off evil influences that we do not have." It was not often when with Lao Tai-tai that I felt any difference in our heritage. And if the thought came to her, "Perhaps it is because of their lesser sensitivity," she did not hold it against me, her friend.

We went outside and sat on the steps of the railless verandah and talked about the way the shrubs and potted plants should be placed, and there we were in complete agreement.

The suggestions my old friend made about the way I should order my house for my better comfort I could parry since they concerned me alone, but there came a suggestion I could neither parry nor withstand.

One morning I found Lao Tai-tai sitting by my desk at the office when I got there, bolt upright as usual and graceful, but with a face more serious than I had ever seen, and a look of strain. Though she tried she could not produce a smile.

"I've brought her to you. I want you to take her."

74

I looked at the young woman standing sulkily behind Lao Tai-tai, holding a little girl of about six by the hand. She was the half-servant, half-ward who had served us the glutinous rice confection Lao Tai-tai and I both liked the first time I had visited Lao Tai-tai and every time since, who had held up the curtain for us when we entered the door of Lao Tai-tai's house, and who had served us tea. She and the little girl lived in Lao Tai-tai's own courtyard, in the West House. Why should Lao Tai-tai be wanting me to take her? The relationship between a mistress and a maid was one of mutual responsibilities with corresponding privileges. The longer a maid was with a mistress the more firmly was she one of the family, the more she would expect to live with the family and be cared for by the family. And this maid had been with Lao Tai-tai since she was seven.

Her father had sold her to Lao Tai-tai to pay his gambling debts, Li Kuan had told me. She was now no longer a slave. Lao Tai-tai, in the tradition of good mistresses, had arranged a marriage for her when she was eighteen or nineteen, had married her to the steward of their property in Manchuria. This was a very good match for the girl, better than she could have expected. When the child was eight months old the husband had died of tuberculosis, and the young woman, now a widow and therefore owning herself and having nowhere else to go, had come back to Lao Tai-tai. In addition to the responsibilities which Lao Tai-tai had discharged by arranging the marriage, there was an affection in Lao Tai-tai's heart for the girl. There was also the willingness she had always had to carry her responsibilities toward others further than demanded by the logic of the pattern. She had let the young woman and her child live in her own courtyard and serve her.

"But I don't understand—" I said.

"You need a maid and you know how well she cooks. She can cook Chinese meals for you. Your cook makes only foreign food."

The last thing I needed was a maidservant. I had planned the house to use men servants only. I preferred men servants. Men servants stayed in their own quarters or in the kitchen when their work was done, but no woman servant could ever see why she should not bring her sewing into whatever room I was sitting in and settle down for a good gossip—or settle down for a good gossip without her sewing. That I was reading or writing did not seem in her eyes to be of consequence, or to make interruptions a nuisance. Nor could she understand that her casual remarks were interruptions.

Lao Tai-tai was right from her point of view. A woman servant was even more a member of the family than a manservant. She was ever present in Chinese families, as present as any part of the living arrangements. She came and went as she pleased. As time went on, and if she was sympathetic, she became practically a part of the family, could take part in family councils and do many of the things a family member usually did. But I had other ideas. I was with people all day long in the hospital. There were people living in the house with me. For lunch or tea or dinner there were guests, and I was often out to lunch or tea, cocktails or dinner. I treasured the few evenings I had at home alone. I liked then to have my dinner in bed, with a pile of books and magazines I had not had time even to look at on the table beside the bed, and settle down for an evening of mental refreshment. I knew this would be difficult with a woman servant. She should be the one to bring the tray, and she would want to talk. I knew my own weakness also, my curiosity about people and the life of people. I knew that I would let her gossip and that my evening of mental refreshment would be gone. There was another consideration concerning this woman. She had been bred in a home of wealth. Even though Lao Tai-tai seemed not to have had great wealth when she was younger, she had had enough to buy a maid. The habits of servants in families of wealth were not habits I wanted in my own home.

"I have not enough work in my small household for another servant," I said.

Lao Tai-tai was persistent. "She can sew for you. She can

learn to cook foreign food and then you will not need a man cook." I knew my cook would not be breaking his own rice bowl by training a possible supplanter.

"There is no place for her to live," I said, trying another gambit. "Lao Li and his wife and little boy have the house in the Servants' Court." Lao Li was the washman-tableboy.

"Oh, she can live in the gatehouse." Lao Tai-tai knew that she had succeeded and her spirits rose. Color began to come into her old-ivory face. The strain, whatever it was, must have been great.

"But that is where the rickshaw boy lives," I said.

"Oh, he can live in the garage. You do not keep a car and the rickshaw does not take up all the space. There's a good window facing east."

So she had been around and studied my compound. The garage with its east window was quite pleasant. It was true the rickshaw boy could live there.

"But the gatehouse faces north," I said. "The maid and the child will get no sunshine, and it is very public to the gate."

"That's all right. It's quite big enough for her and the child, and they will be in it nights only."

I sighed inside. She would be enjoying the sunshine in my living room all through the day; and why should she not? She could have it all day long while I was away. But would she leave it to me when I came back in the afternoon?

"I cannot pay her much. You know my scale of wages. Guests to Western homes do not tip. She will have to cook her own food and that of the child, and pay for it out of her own wages." In my home, unlike Chinese homes, there was no central kitchen from which all in the house could eat.

"That's all right," said Lao Tai-tai. "I'll take her right over and wait until you come home for lunch, when we'll fix up her room for her. I'll see that she lacks nothing."

My old friend was asking me a favor, one that obviously meant a great deal to her, and I had no real reason for refusing. It would be a sad world where we could not put ourselves out occasionally for our friends. The door of the gatehouse was moved from the passageway to the courtyard, making it a bit less public, and Ho Chieh and her six-year-old daughter moved in.

There were now more servants than I needed, so the work was never done as well as it should be done, each thinking the other was not taking his share; and the peaceful harmony of the pattern that had begun to be established in my home was disturbed, never to run as smoothly again.

Yang, the cook, would not let Ho Chieh cook or even watch him cook for fear she would learn his trade and supplant him. Grudgingly, once in a while, he would let her serve me a Chinese meal, since he was not a cook of Chinese food. Lao Li was only too glad to let her wait on table. But she could never learn to do it according to our pattern, could never do anything twice in succession the same way. Evenings when we had guests the boy had to put on his long white gown and serve while she acted as second boy, giving me a two-boy household prestige I did not want. Sometimes I thought I saw Ho Chieh enjoying watching the rickshaw puller sweep the courtyards, knowing she could not be asked to help. And she hated to sew or to clean up the rooms or even to make the beds. And so I had one more servant to share the work that was already light for the three men, and with difficulty got done any of the work a maid should have done.

Still, Ho Chieh told me stories of Lao Tai-tai's life, though not as many as I could have wished. It was not easy to touch her imagination, and she was often surly.

Lao Tai-tai came more often to my house and I was glad of that. Sometimes she came to see me but always she came to see this young woman, who was almost one of her daughters. Sometimes when I had come in through the Great Gate, opened for me by Ho Chieh, and was passing through the Entrance Court, I would see the tips of Lao Tai-tai's feet swinging over the edge of the bed in Ho Chieh's room. I would go on to my part of the house, knowing that if Lao Tai-tai wanted to see me she would come into the inner court, whereas if she wanted to see Ho Chieh only, I was supposed not to know that she had been there.

On Ho Chieh's chest of drawers was a picture of Lao Tai-tai. It showed her as a young matron, dressed in the tight sleeves and flaring high collar, the tight coat with the flair at the knees, and the long tight trousers that had been so fashionable in the early years of the Republic. The same vividness was in the pictured face that was in her face now, when she was already counted an old woman. The same eyes looked out directly at whatever there was to be seen, to be appraised, to be enjoyed.

Li Kuan told me why Lao Tai-tai had had to send Ho Chieh away. "Ho Chieh quarreled with the Second Master's concubine. She has an obstinate disposition and was foolish enough to match words with one of the family. The Second Master came to Lao Tai-tai and said, 'Either that woman leaves or I and my wife leave.' You know he is her favorite son. I think that if it had been the Third Master she might have let him go." But the Third Master would never have made that demand.

Also I learned in time from experience why the Second Master's concubine had not wanted Ho Chieh in the same compound with her.

CHAPTER 9

At last something happened to break through Ho Chieh's inertia and set her to talking about Lao Tai-tai's youth. I took advantage of the opportunity and asked many questions. I have wondered why I did not ask Lao Tai-tai herself these questions. I am sure she would have been glad to tell me the stories. I have come to the conclusion that we never had time when we were together. The present was always too interesting and too much alive, and the plans for the future too important, for Lao Tai-tai or anyone with her to dwell on the past.

Ho Chieh brought my dinner on the tray and set it on the bedside table and then squatted on the floor by the door. It was the most comfortable way for her to sit. I saw the glint in her eyes as she said, "The Second Master's little wife has another son." "Little wife" was a not so polite way to speak of a concubine living in the family home.

"That makes three, doesn't it? One a year?"

"Four children in five years—the second was a girl."

I nodded and picked up the magazine on top of the pile on the table.

"The Second Master says the child is to carry the surname of his own father."

"But the surname of the Second Master's father is Yin," I said, stating what I thought was the obvious.

"Oh no, the Second Master and his sister 'came over' with Lao Tai-tai when she married the Old Master."

I dropped the magazine. There could be nothing on its pages as interesting as this. Lao Tai-tai married twice! According to the pattern widows were not supposed to remarry. Ho Chieh had said "come over," which could mean only that she had remarried and brought her children with her to her second husband. "To come over," to accompany the mother to her new home in a second marriage, was common enough in poor families, where widows remarried to have something to eat and for their children to eat, but a second marriage among the well-to-do was not common. And what kind of family was it that gave up a son? Even in poor families the sons were usually kept and only the daughters sent away with the mother. Sometimes families with means used pretexts to do what they wanted to do. There was the widow of substance (near my old home in Shantung) who wanted to marry a widower of substance. Her grown sons and his grown sons conspired to have her kidnapped when on a journey, then rescued and taken to the man's home for refuge. After passing a night in a man's home, what could she do but marry him?

But Ho Chieh was going on with the story. "They have not always been rich. Also there were none of her husband's people in this part of the country." To claim the son, Ho Chieh meant. "So when Lao Tai-tai remarried she took her own two small children over with her—the Eldest Daughter and the one who is now called the Second Master of the Yin Family." Ho Chieh was squatting comfortably by the door, prepared for a good gossip. "Lao Tai-tai's first husband's surname was Hsu, and he was from Shansi Province. Now that they are wealthy the Second Master wants to honor his own ancestors. He went to Shansi last year and looked up his relatives. So this new Little Master—his third son by the concubine—will have the surname Hsu and worship the Hsu ancestors."

"But why doesn't the Second Master himself take the surname Hsu?" I asked. Having been brought up and having made his career with his stepfather's name it would not be easy, I knew, to change over to another, but the question was a way to keep Ho Chieh talking.

"Oh, he could not do that. He would lose his destiny—his good fortune. That is why he waited for the third son to honor the Hsu Family. The first two as well as Little Root must continue the Yin line. All know that the Yin Family wealth is due to the good vein in the earth where the Old Master's mother is buried."

Where the parents were buried was considered to be of great importance to the prosperity of the family for many generations. Families often spent large sums in getting the best geomancers to locate the best possible places for burying their parents. An unfortunate burying place could bring bad luck for generations.

"Old Master Yin's family was very poor when he was a child." Ho Chieh was fairly launched on her story. "He was the only son of a widow. When he was seven years old the Long Haired Ones came through his home district."

The Long Haired Ones was what people called the soldiers of the Taiping Army because they refused to shave the inch back of the hairline around their heads and braid their hair as did those who were a part of the Manchu Empire. Instead they let all their hair grow long and combed it in the old Chinese way, as during the Ming Dynasty (a purely Chinese dynasty), into a knot on the top of the head. In battle this knot would come undone, and their hair flying like a banner from the tops of their heads made them even more terrifying to the people. Sometimes the people called them the Long Haired Bandits. What did the people know of empires and dynasties, of modernization and of the outside world? They knew, in some parts of the country, that there had been a dream of deliverance from the burden of taxation, from the heavy concentrations of land in a few families, from foreign interference. But all knew that war devastated, that their homes were burned, their crops ruined, their men killed and their women carried off. Not all who called themselves Taipings were soldiers fighting for the people.

"His mother seized him by the hand and fled toward the hills," Ho Chieh went on. "They hid behind a bank to wait until the bandits had passed." It was hard on women who were caught by the "bandits." The plain ones were made to carry food and loads for the soldiers. Women of that province did not have bound feet unless they were wealthy, and the Old Master and his mother were poor. The well-favored were taken by the bandits for their women, and the beautiful ones were sent to their princes.

"As the bandits were passing, his mother pulled him down behind the bank. But he was a child. He heard the gongs beating and saw the red banners waving. He cried out, 'Pretty, pretty.' The bandits heard and captured them. They placed a pole on the woman's shoulders, for she had had smallpox and was ill-favored to look upon, and made her carry pails of rice.

"When she came to a ditch with water in it, she jumped into the ditch and drowned herself. When the bandits looked around, they said, "Where is the woman we caught this morning? She was carrying the pails." Then they saw the pails standing on the side of the ditch, and when they looked down they saw her feet sticking up out of the water. For the water was not deep.

"A nephew also had been captured. He was a man of learning and so had been made a secretary to the prince. He came and bought a coffin and placed her in it and buried her there in the ditch where she had drowned herself. That ditch was in a good vein of the earth. Her grave there has had good influence on the family fortunes. The family has prospered."

"What happened to the little boy?" I asked.

"The little boy was taken to the prince, and he became the adopted son of the prince. He was very beautiful. He lived with the prince of the bandits for ten years."

I remembered the story Lao Tai-tai had told of the little princeling and the beautiful girl who hanged herself.

"Then what happened?"

Ho Chieh smiled. She was actually enjoying herself. "When Li Hung-chang defeated the Taipings he took the Old Master— he was about seventeen then—and brought him up in his new army. He liked the Old Master and the Old Master was also from Anhwei Province."

I knew Li Hung-chang's reputation for surrounding himself with men of his own province, Anhwei. Li Hung-chang was one of the great ministers who served during the last years of the Manchu Dynasty. He had helped to put down the Taiping

Rebellion, that first stuttering effort of the people to free themselves from that dynasty (which according to the historical lifespan of dynasties should have ended then) and from the encroaching imperialism of the West. For more than half a century he had worked for the dying dynasty and helped to prolong its useless life. He had seen clearly the weakness of the old empire and told the young men around him, those he was training for official life, "China is a tiger painted on paper." He saw the weakness of the old empire but tried to strengthen his country against the encroachments of the "Powers," to save China from the partitions so talked about at that time. "China is hopeless," the Powers had said; "we must take her over for her own good" and the good of our pocketbooks. This last, however, was not said out loud. With his able diplomacy and the modern army he was building, with officers from abroad to train his troops, Li Hung-chang, more than any other one person, had kept China together during the second half of the nineteenth century, while at the same time he had saved the Manchu Dynasty.

"So the Old Master was an army officer. How did he come to marry Lao Tai-tai, who was from Manchuria? Li Hung-chang's model troops were in a village near Tientsin." Again I thought I was stating the obvious. Was not Lao Tai-tai's brother in Manchuria? Had not the family moved here from Manchuria?

"No," Ho Chieh settled herself more firmly on her heels. "No, Lao Tai-tai's family are not from Manchuria. They moved there later. They lived in the village outside Tientsin, the barracks village where Li Hung-chang had his troops."

Families of consequence did not live in barracks towns. This was another proof of Lao Tai-tai's comparatively humble origin.

"Lao Tai-tai was the most beautiful girl in the village. All the young men in the village wanted to marry her."

That was easy to believe. I was sure the matchmakers met each other coming and going across her father's doorstep.

"The Old Master," and I knew Ho Chieh was talking about Old Master Yin, "wanted to marry her." Then, seeing that I was about to ask another question, Ho Chieh went on, "Her father ran a little store that sold groceries—grain, salt, vinegar, oil. It was not a large store. The mother helped manage it. She was, like Lao Tai-tai, able to get things done, but she was not pleasant as Lao Tai-tai always is. Sometimes she would visit Lao Tai-tai. I did not like her. You have seen the brother. You know what kind of family they are." Ho Chieh stopped a moment and thought. "Even the brother's family are not quite the same now. They are more prosperous. The Second Master helped his uncle—his mother's brother—to set up a larger business."

I had seen this brother of Lao Tai-tai's—a small-town businessman. Intelligent enough, he would never have the polished city look of the Second Master. He would always look like a man whose days were spent with routine details and in a small place. I wondered where Lao Tai-tai had acquired her perfection of manner, a way of acting that did not seem to be manner at all, so natural and gracious it was. If Lao Tai-tai's father kept a store in a garrison town, neither the wealth of the family nor their social position could have been great.

"The Old Master saw her in her father's shop and wanted to marry her."

In my imagination I could see the long village street lined on either side with the open-front shops that catered to the army, selling groceries, grain, and cloth, and the wine shops, and the shops that sold goods for the horses—saddles studded with shining brass, bridles, whips, decorated stirrups. I could see their own shop with its open front so that all who passed by could see the foodstuffs and smell the sesame oil and peanut oil, the spices in their jars on the shelves, the tea in the wooden boxes. There would be a counter running two-thirds of the way across the shop. The Old Man and his wife would stand behind it and, helped by their children, would serve the customers. The Old Man, however, was more likely to be sitting on the bench by the threshold, near the grain bins, waiting to welcome his customers. They probably had an apprentice or two. As the girl grew they would try to keep her more and more in the background, away from the eyes of men. But I could not imagine Lao Tai-tai at any age not looking with bright eyes at all that came within range, even if at times, when still a maiden, she would let the heavy eyelids droop.

The young officer had seen her in the shop, but perhaps also he had seen her on festival days when all went to visit the temples and could not but jostle each other, the crowds were so great and packed so tightly. Perhaps the officers staged horse shows and she sat with her family in one of the booths made of straw matting and set up by the side of the track, while the officers rode by on their pacing horses, each trying to make a better showing than the last in his style of sitting in the saddle, in the material and trimmings of the saddle blankets and the silver or copper mountings of the saddle. Perhaps he had seen her when the stock companies came to town and put up their mat-shed stage on someone's threshing floor, or perhaps on the drill ground, and all turned out to watch and listen to the play that was more an opera than a play. Lao Tai-tai would be with her mother and the other women on the edge of the crowd. They would have benches to sit on but would probably stand on them to see over the heads of the men standing in the crowd around the stage.

"But her father would not give her to him," Ho Chieh went on, "to a soldier thirteen years older than she."

"How old was she then?"

"About sixteen."

That was two counts against the man—to be much older and to be a soldier. For the first marriage it was thought best for the boy and girl to be about the same age, or for there to be a difference of a couple of years only, with the girl the older. This would be a difference in ages greater than anyone liked. It was usual also for self-respecting tradesmen to look down on soldiers. Even if the Old Man himself belonged to the lowest of the four respectable classes in society—the scholar, the farmer, the craftsman, and the merchant—he was still higher than the soldier, whose sons could not enter the examinations which were the gateway to political posts, rich offices, and honor. Even if her father had been progressive enough—and that was doubtful—to see that Li Hung-chang was trying to build a modern army so that China could take her place in a modern world, he still would not be willing to accept a soldier as an equal.

Lao Tai-tai had been a girl of her times, when as a matter of course the family arranged the marriages of their children, and probably had not questioned her father's decisions. Since she was a girl of sixteen, it was hard to know how deeply her emotions were involved, or if they were involved at all.

"Lao Tai-tai's father married her to a man from Shansi, to a pawnbroker named Hsu."

This was a marriage in her own class, to another tradesman. Perhaps it was a step up, in the Old Man's mind at least. The pawnbrokers of Shansi Province were noted for their ability to acquire wealth. Pawnbrokers were the bankers of the period—they and the grain shop keepers.

That it could not have been too large a town where they lived Ho Chieh's next words proved. "The Old Master then picked out the second most beautiful girl in town and married her."

This would seem to be final—a doubly complicated triangle. There was no divorce in old China except that a man might send his wife back to her people if she had seriously misbehaved. But if she had a family to protect her, he had better be very sure of her misbehavior or her brother would engage him in such a series of lawsuits that he might well be ruined.

"But the Old Master's life was controlled by the good influences of his mother's grave—see how rich the Second Master has become. He was a baby, of course, when he and his older sister followed Lao Tai-tai, when she married Old Master Yin."

"You are going too fast," I interrupted Ho Chieh. "The Old Master was married to the second most—"

"Oh, she died when the boy was born. He's the one at the old home in Anhwei Province, the one they call the First Master."

"The one who is not very bright," I said. I was glad that this not very bright son had not been born of Lao Tai-tai.

"Yes, he lives in the Old Home. The Family sent him to the police college in Tientsin, but he could not hold a job. All he's good for is to sit on the land and eat tile-bread, eat rents."

"The brains came from Lao Tai-tai's side of the family," I said. "It's the Second Master who has made the money." Then I remembered that he had had a Shansi pawnbroker for a father, which also might have had something to do with his abilities.

"Yes," said Ho Chieh, "the Second Master has brains, but the good fortune comes from the grave of the Old Master's mother."

"So when they were married he already had a son and she had a son and a daughter—"

"And after they were married to each other they had three children. The Third Master is like the Old Man, but he is not as handsome, or as intelligent or charming. The Fourth Master and the daughter are like Lao Tai-tai." Ho Chieh thought a moment. "The Fourth Master has both Lao Tai-tai's and the Old Master's good looks and charm."

"So Lao Tai-tai and the Old Master were very fond of each other," I said, to bring Ho Chieh back to the main story.

"Yes, the Old Master loved Lao Tai-tai all the time. When the Second Master was a baby and her husband died, the Old Master came and asked her to marry him."

As a widow she could dispose of her own hand, even in the old days. A widow was not supposed to remarry, but many did. The most usual reason was of course that she was poor and had no other way to eat or feed her children. Sometimes necessity was used as an excuse, when there was no actual poverty. Lao Tai-tai also was far from her husband's family, and there were none of his people to claim the baby son.

"Just before they were married the Old Master had an accident. You have seen his picture, and that one eye was different." I nodded.

"He was blind in that eye and it was all because of Lao Tai-tai. One of the cannons blew up. They were having a celebration in the camp and fired off many guns. The one the Old Master was firing blew up. It exploded and a piece of iron flew into the Old Master's eye. He went to a doctor. The doctor told him that the injury was serious but that he thought the eye could be saved if the Old Master took his medicine and abstained from women for three months.

"But the Old Master said, 'I cannot do that. I am about to marry the woman I once lost.'

"He loved her very much. When they were already old and I came back to live with them again, and even until his last days, he could not let her pass his chair without putting out his arm and touching her. He would draw her to his lap and say, 'Is she not a fine woman? Was it not worth losing an eye for her?' "

CHAPTER 10

Two of Lao Tai-tai's visits, more frequent now that Ho Chieh lived with us, stand out in my mind.

One day when she came into the inner courtyard to see me, Ning Lao Tai-tai, my other old friend, was already there. Perhaps that was why Yin Lao Tai-tai came in that day, as much to see this other old women about whom Ho Chieh had most certainly told her as to see me—this other old woman whose life had begun, to outward appearances, so nearly on the same level as hers and was now so different. Both had been born into shopkeeping families; but where Ning Lao Tai-tai's father had failed in the business of selling salt, vinegar, sauce, and spices, Yin Lao Tai-tai's father had become moderately well-to-do while selling these and other things. Ning Lao Tai-tai's opium-smoking husband had lost his farmland and his fishing boat, and Yin Lao Tai-tai's husband had been a successful if minor official. Although Ning Lao Tai-tai had once been a beggar and had spent most of her life as a serving woman, and Yin Lao Tai-tai had never in her life been in want and now ruled a great compound with many men and women servants, they met as equals and talked as equals.

It was a warm day in early spring. We were sitting in the courtyard by the "pagoda trees" (the pine trees that grew so tall, with limbs so tightly growing upward) to get the afternoon sunshine, still pleasant to feel. Lao Li (the washman-tableboy) was busy tearing the paper from the upper half of the latticed windows and pasting on the gauze that would keep out the flies in the summer-that-was-coming and let the breezes through. Ning Lao Tai-tai had a big rush basket on her lap and another on the ground beside her as she sorted over the mulberry leaves she had plucked in my back garden to feed the silkworms she was raising. The branches of the elm tree across the courtyard swayed against the blue sky and the swing of the grey tiled roofs. The tiny elm blossoms fell on the ground and the corner of the balcony like chartreuse snow. We were talking about the different ways these "elm tree cash," as they were called—because they were yellow and round and had a tiny hole in the middle like the copper coins the Chinese had used until the 1911 Revolution—could be used in making "spring cakes." They were laid between layers of dough made of cornmeal and millet ground fine and raised with yeast, and then steamed.

Suddenly the little dogs, black or golden-brown or honey-colored, sprang from where they lay on the bricks around our feet, bounded across the court, and poured barking over the threshold of the Second Gate. They came back soberly escorting Yin Lao Tai-tai. They would not bark at her.

We sat in the courtyard and chatted until Ho Chieh announced that tea was ready. She had laid it on the table in the dining room across the court. As I walked behind my two friends I wondered how they would settle the matter of precedence, of who should sit in the higher seat. The seats of honor were those opposite the door. To these I would usher them. The one on the left, however, was higher than the one on the right. Which would take it, and on what basis would they make their decision?

The cut of their clothes was not too different. Both were dressed in knee-length coats and trousers bound in at the ankles, conservative clothes as befitted their age, but while Yin Lao Tai-tai's were of grey silk and smartly cut, Ning Lao Tai-tai's were of black sateen and wider and more clumsy in their cut. Both women were evidently in their sixties. Yin Lao Tai-tai's hair, almost white, was combed back smoothly over her head and knotted at her neck, while Ning Lao Tai-tai's hair did not lie as smoothly on her head but showed very little grey. One's face was as smooth as a young girl's; the other's was crossed with many lines and grooves made by suffering and by laughter. The one had the air of command and resources about her, the other the unselfconscious self-respect of a woman who had done all her life what she had had to do and had enjoyed life in spite of everything.

I listened as they talked. They were going to settle it by age.

"How old are you?" This was Yin Lao Tai-tai, and she used the formal polite phrase for asking this question, which was always one of the first asked.

"Sixty-eight. And how old are you?"

Yin Lao Tai-tai could claim sixty-one only, so Ning Lao Tai-tai was placed in the higher seat of honor as befitted her greater number of years.

At the table they chatted and sparred.

"And how many sons have you?"

"I have four." Yin Lao Tai-tai had a right to hold her head a fraction higher than she always held it. Four sons was "blessing" indeed. "And how many have you?"

"I have only one," said Ning Lao Tai-tai, looking slightly depressed. "And how many grandsons have you?" She was carrying on the traditional questioning.

"I have only one." Yin Lao Tai-tai, with the courtesy and tact of her people, had neglected to mention the sons born to her Second Son's concubine. She must have been forearmed by Ho Chieh with all the vital information about Ning Lao Tai-tai's family. "How many have you?"

"I have four," said Ning Lao Tai-tai proudly, and the score was even.

Then there was the day Lao Tai-tai saw Philip.

Lao Tai-tai and I were sitting in the big wicker chairs in the shaded corner of the courtyard, watching Lao Li feed the cats and the dogs. Each of the five cats had a plate on the window ledge, and each of the seven dogs had a plate on the verandah floor. The afternoon sun burnished the coats of these little animals, who were all about the same size, black and brown for the little Pekingese dogs, honey-colored for the Tibetan lion dog Lao Tai-tai had given me, and white and orange for the cats. It was amusing to watch the serene unconcern with which the cats slowly ate while the little dogs each ran from plate to plate, afraid one of the others had something better than he.

I had been telling Lao Tai-tai about how my rooms had, one by one, become occupied. There was Hui Chen, a young woman from my staff at the hospital, who was now living in the guest suite in the outer courtyard; also Bob, a young American working with the Famine Relief Society, and Francis, a young Chinese on my staff, were living in the East House, where my study had been turned into another bedroom. I knew Lao Tai-tai was pleased that I had moved back to the Main House. Moreover, when the two girls at boarding school were home to occupy the Ear Houses, at last I had my bed in the correct place for the Master's bed.

Lao Tai-tai turned her head when she heard the quick light steps coming through the Second Gate. Following her eyes I turned also to see Philip crossing the courtyard. Lao Tai-tai's eyes widened with interest as he swung down the path with his free island stride. When he stopped to greet me I introduced him.

"Bob said to wait for him. You'll find the papers on his desk."

"Who is he?" said Lao Tai-tai as soon as Philip was safely in the house. "He's a very likely-looking young man. That's better than being handsome. He is intelligent and able. Is he married?"

I told her that Philip was from Honolulu; that he had come to study in one of the Peking universities in order to learn the ways of his own motherland; that he was earning his way through college by guiding tourists through the imperial palaces and parks, many of which were now open to the public; that he and Bob were good friends; and that Bob was helping him work out the text of some leaflets to distribute through the hotels where the tourists stayed. When I said that he was not married, not even engaged, Lao Tai-tai said, "I think he would make a good husband for my granddaughter. Will you be the go-between—speak to him for me?"

Well as I knew Lao Tai-tai, I could still be surprised by her directness and quickness of decision, but her shrewd sense had not erred. I knew Philip was a young man any grandmother would be glad to have marry her granddaughter. I realized that her ever-busy mind was always on the watch for opportunities to further the interests of any member of her family. It was time also, according to traditional ways, that arrangements should be made for the marriage of the Little Mistress.

That Philip was an Overseas Chinese, to my surprise, made no difference to Lao Tai-tai, nor that he was of Southern stock. Most Northerners looked down on the Southerners, considered it natural to do so. Northerners were Sons of Han, naming themselves from the Han Dynasty (206 B.C.–A.D. 264), when China had first become a world power and reached the first great rise in her culture; while the people of the South, from Kwangtung Province, called themselves men of T'ang, naming themselves from the T'ang Dynasty (A.D. 619–906), when many parts of the South had joined the Empire. The Overseas Chinese are from the southern provinces, of stock that had been late, only a thousand years or so ago, coming into the Chinese cultural pattern. The Overseas Chinese, living in countries not their own, were not educated in the Chinese classics, most of them could not read their own ancestral language, and they spoke the local patois of the region from which their ancestors had come.

Philip was flattered when I placed the proposal before him, and also tempted. It was not easy to work his way through college and get a footing in Peking with neither family nor funds to back him; but the differences between the cultures in which he and the girl had been brought up, though their racial heritage was the same, held him back. "I wouldn't know the first thing about how to act in her family," he said, "—all those little everyday things. Tell Lao Tai-tai that I am not worthy to enter her family and that I have not yet graduated. If in a year, when I have graduated, she still wants me, we can talk it over again."

That he would have become one of Lao Tai-tai's family instead of the girl joining his was one of the things that held energetic Philip back, as well as the fact that he had never met the girl, who was still very young. It was a well-known pattern for a poor boy of ability to be taken into a wealthy family as a son-in-law.

Lao Tai-tai understood that Philip was grateful and honored but not yet ready to tie himself down, and did not push the matter. She always took a lively interest in him, however, and they became good friends.

CHAPTER 11

O n one of my visits to Lao Tai-tai's home I had been surprised to see her young daughter's hair cut short like that of a student. It was becoming, but I missed the long heavy braid of shining black hair. This youngest of Lao Tai-tai's children, this girl who was now about twenty years old, I now realized was one about whom I knew very little. Always courteous to us, she would help the maid serve her mother's guests with tea and cakes and sit at the table and eat with us the delicacies Lao Tai-tai set before us; but she had always seemed withdrawn, as though she would rather be back in her own room, the one beyond Lao Tai-tai's. Even with us she was thinking her own thoughts and not interested in what we were saying.

I now began to wonder what those thoughts would have been. I had taken for granted that she was a conventional girl of a wealthy family, interested in her clothes and studying perhaps with a tutor, perhaps preparing her trousseau as girls of her age had done when I was growing up in Shantung Province. She was of an age soon to marry. I now realized that it had been the long black braid which had labeled her and placed her in my mind as a conventional daughter in a wealthy home. Now that her hair was cut across her neck and dressed as a student in a middle school or college would dress her hair, I looked at her with other eyes. What, after all, did I know of her? Perhaps she was going out to school every day, as was her young niece, Little Root's sister. Ever since I had known them Little Root's sister's hair had been cut short while this girl's had been long. That she had cut it now meant, I was sure, that something definite had happened.

She had not smiled at me as she greeted me that day. I was her mother's friend; how could I know anything about what had made her revolt? I was now sure that the short hair was a sign of revolt. I could see the determination in the girl's face, a determination that left no place for sullenness. There was a purpose in the young face that made it look even more like the old face. My mind went back, and I remembered expressions on the girl's face that I had not thought about at the time.

"The young daughter is giving Lao Tai-tai much trouble," said Li Kuan when I told her I had been to see the family. "It's a question of the marriage. She wants to marry her cousin."

The word Li Kuan had used for cousin was the one used for mother's brother's son. Cousins of the same surname were counted as brothers and sisters. Marriage between them would be counted incest and so impossible. However, for a girl to marry into the same family into which her father's sister had married was considered very good indeed. Such a marriage made the girl's mother-in-law her own aunt, who would therefore treat her better, it was believed, than an ordinary mother-in-law. It would be "going forward" with the aunt, going into the same family the aunt had gone into. Marriages between such cousins were sought. I had never heard, however, of a marriage backward, so to speak, of a girl going back to her own mother's people. Perhaps a mere uncle—even a mother's brother, who had so much responsibility for his sister's children (clothing them when they were small, ensuring that they were educated or learned trades)—was not supposed to be able to secure good treatment from an alien woman as mother-in-law. It was evident, though, that this could and did happen.

"Lao Tai-tai does not like the boy—thinks he is not steady enough. He is a student in one of the Tientsin colleges. He is very active with the guerillas and in working politically against the Japanese. Lao Tai-tai is not very politically-minded, you know. She thinks it is wrong for the Japanese to be in Manchuria, that it is not according to the logic of the pattern of that which is right for one people to do to another people; but she thinks it is a job of the soldiers to drive them out. It is not for students who could become officials to do that kind of work. She thinks he will never make a fortune."

So the girl must have been going to school in Tientsin, and that was why she had not been in Lao Tai-tai's room to greet us during the last year or two.

"What is Lao Tai-tai going to do about it?" I asked, thinking of the strength in the young face so like what the old one must have been at her age, and of the glint in the young eyes when any of us said anything with which she as a young modern Chinese could not agree; and of the look of strain in Lao Tai-tai's face.

"Lao Tai-tai says she is not going to have anything to do with the matter. She is leaving everything to her sons, to the girl's brothers."

In this matter the Fourth Master would be an ally. I did not think he was politically-minded, but he had made an unconventional marriage himself.

"I remember the boy's father was here a while back. Perhaps it was about this affair."

"No, Lao Tai-tai is very fond of her brother and they consult about most things. The old people can do nothing about this matter. They are afraid to try. The girl is very strong-willed and so is the boy."

"Seems to run in the family," I murmured.

"And there is destiny," Li Kuan ignored my interruption. "Destiny crossed makes trouble for all until it is uncrossed. Sometimes that means years of unhappiness."

I nodded. No matter how a philosophy is phrased or what philosophic structure has been built up by any group, it is a human fact that when people are kept from doing what they have to do, there is likely to be trouble of one kind or another.

"Lao Tai-tai says, 'If they must go their own way, they must go their own way.' You see, there was her own trouble when her father would not let her marry the Old Master when she was very young, and there was the trouble with her older daughter when she and the Old Master tried to make her marry his son. So now Lao Tai-tai is not willing to be too severe in the matter of a marriage."

"And what was the trouble with the First Daughter?" I asked.

Here was another element in Lao Tai-tai's life I had never heard about.

"When Lao Tai-tai 'went over,'" (and I knew Li Kuan meant by the term "went over" when she left the Hsu Family to marry into the Yin Family—this would be the way it was thought of even if neither of the families were around when she remarried and it had been a personal matter between her and the Old Master) "she had a daughter and a son, and the Old Master had a son—"

I nodded. I knew that part of the story.

"They knew how difficult it is to bring up other people's children." The unhappy stepchild is as prominent a figure in Chinese folk tales as in those of the old European cultures. "They said, 'We will not quarrel about our children. We will give no one an opportunity to say that we are partial each to our own children.' So they decided to marry her daughter to his son. They engaged the children to each other when very small. The Old Master said, 'Your daughter shall marry my son. I will be the inside father-in-law to your daughter and you will be the outside mother-in-law to my son, and there will be no step-parents.'

"But the two children grew up hating each other. The girl was three years older than the boy and much more intelligent. The boy was slow. She called him stupid. There was a tutor for the children. When the boy went at noon for his food, the girl went in to study. She would not enter the schoolroom if he was there. When he came back she would go away again. If they met they quarreled.

"But they were engaged. It was a family settlement. When the propitious day was chosen they dressed her in her bridal robes." Li Kuan began to laugh. "You have seen her. Lao Tai-tai says she looks like her Shansi father and was no more beautiful then than she is now.

"The girl wept and stormed, said the boy was stupid and that she would not marry him. The boy sulked and said that the girl was ugly and that he would not marry her. The Old Master and Lao Tai-tai loved each other so much they could not imagine their children not loving each other. They thought the young people were just acting up as children do.

"They had the wedding procession and the wedding feast. They shut the two young people up together in the bridal room. The next morning when they opened the doors they saw the boy sitting in one corner of the room and the girl in another with their backs to each other, sulking. At last Lao Tai-tai and the Old Master knew that the marriage would not work. They had much trouble getting another husband for the girl."

Having spent a night in a room with a man, though it was evident they had not been near each other, technically she was a married woman and no longer a virgin. Furthermore she was one discarded by her husband. She was damaged goods.

Li Kuan went on. "When the family moved to another province they married her to a tradesman in the village and the Old Master paid him much money, enough to enlarge his shop. But she had stayed a widow in her mother's house for many years before that happened."

This was the hard-faced woman I had seen one day when I was visiting Lao Tai-tai. She had come out of the Third Master's House to greet me. She looked older than her mother. She did not look as though she were even related to Lao Tai-tai. I was not surprised that Lao Tai-tai had not loved this woman's father, the Shansi pawnbroker.

CHAPTER 12

Oone afternoon Ho Chieh did not come to open the gate
with the slow step and the dragging walk that so an-
noyed me. She came with a quick, springing step of which I
had been sure she was capable. I could hear the slap of her
cloth-soled shoes and the click of her leather heels as she crossed
the court and came into the gate-cave. When she caught up
with me after sliding the gate-bolt to, and the barking of the little dogs who had poured out to meet me had subsided, she
said, "Shall I serve tea in the courtyard or in the living room?"
This was unusual. Usually she stood around until I asked her
to bring the tea and then told her where to serve it.

When she had the tea table set and the tea poured, and had
watched me drink enough, as she estimated, to refresh me, she
said, "My father is here."

"Your father! Did he not sell you? You do not belong to his
family?"

"Yes, he sold me, and I no longer belong to his family, but he
is my father."

That was what I expected her to say. The father had raised
money on his daughter as he would on any negotiable property, but that was a matter of a few years only. The family relationship was eternal. In fact, having sale value was one of the
qualities of being a daughter and a filial daughter. I was also
prepared for Ho Chieh's next remark.

"He wants you to find him a job."

Among the many activities of the Social Service Department
in the big hospital, that of getting work for our patients was the
one perhaps we most enjoyed. It was good to see a family beginning to live again after having existed only. It was good,
when we got the man a job, to see the children's faces become

rosy. It was good, when we got a woman work, to see her face begin to fill out and hope come into her eyes. Others besides our patients came to us to find work. But we were not magicians. We could not create work, and work opportunities were becoming more and more scarce. Raw materials were being drained from our part of the country to Tientsin to feed the Japanese mills; mechanized industry was beginning to dispossess those who worked in the handicrafts; and furthermore, since the mechanized industry had been brought into the country by foreigners, the profits went abroad instead of being spent in the country. These changes in industry meant also changes in the ways of living for the people. As in all such changes, there are those who lose their work, and there was no planning being done to take those who were dispossessed into other kinds of work. But we in the Social Service had a reputation for getting work for people. I knew, however, that what Ho Chieh wanted for her father was not a job in the new industry or in the old, but a sinecure—assistant gate-keeper, perhaps, to take the telephone calls or carry an occasional message. That was the traditional way to care for the old or the useless in the structure of the old agricultural-handicraft society. I had seen these pensioned old men playing chess under the ancient trees in the Entrance Courts of the palaces of the dispossessed Manchu princes, keeping the gates while their masters waited for someone to come and buy the palaces so that they might eat a while longer. I had seen these old men keeping the gates in the homes of my friends.

"It does not matter what kind of job you get him—enough for him to eat will do."

How often I had heard that phrase—"Enough to eat will do."

"How long is he going to stay?"

"Until he finds a job."

Ho Chieh meant that if I did not get him a position he would stay with her and eat her food, and that meant that my bills would go up. Also I knew he would be underfoot and distract the other servants. Was he not a gambler? Was not gambling an almost universal pastime? I shrewdly suspected my cook of running a gambling outfit in his own home further down the street from where I lived. It seemed a larger house than was necessary for his family, and gambling was a traditional occupation for the cooks of Peking. They handled the right amount of fluid money to finance small-scale gambling that ran into large-scale gambling. I had heard lately that my cook had been made an officer of the Cook's Guild. That could mean more forms of gambling. I did not want to increase his activities further or have any of them moved over to my house.

"Did he not sell you when you were very small?" I was trying to see how strong was her filial piety. Also I had a point to make.

"He could not care for me. We had nothing to eat. My mother was sick on the kang. There was nothing left to sell but me."

"Was there not also the matter of the gambling debts?"

"He will always gamble—as long as he lives."

Ho Chieh and I looked at each other, and we understood each other. It was accepted by all that a man who gambled was not a good risk as a servant of any kind. She knew that I would not be able to recommend him to anyone, and that furthermore the relationship between her and me was not yet of long enough duration to require me to go beyond her and her child in my responsibility toward her. She knew also that I would not be hard on her or on her father.

The father stayed in my compound the better part of a month—a faded nondescript figure that flitted through the gate into the servants' quarters when I came into the Entrance Court. Then I saw him no more. I suspected that Lao Tai-tai had been able to find him that sinecure. Perhaps, if I had known which of her friends she had persuaded to take him, I would have seen him sweeping out one of the courts when she and her friends were around to see him do it, without much productive activity at any other time.

The relationship between Lao Tai-tai and Ho Chieh was a deep one, one of many years that entailed the responsibilities of many years. Not only had Lao Tai-tai secured the place for Ho Chieh and the child in my home, she came often to see her and always brought her money. I never enquired in which bank was Ho Chieh's growing account. To Lao Tai-tai—as to every good Chinese—every privilege had its responsibilities and every responsibility its privileges.

"I was only seven or eight when Lao Tai-tai took me," Ho Chieh had said to me. "I do not remember much. We stood by the side of the road—my father and I. Lao Tai-tai came riding by on a little furry donkey. She was young then. She was dressed in fine clothes. She got off her donkey and asked my father what he was doing with me, standing by the side of the road. So she bought me from my father."

CHAPTER 13

A friend of mine from Japan was visiting me and so enjoyed my modest garden that I wanted her to see Lao Tai-tai's. I knew my friend was one who would recognize Lao Tai-tai's quality and love her, see in her the best in the old Chinese pattern.

I asked my secretary to telephone to the Yin household and find out when it would be convenient for us to call. On the day set the three of us got into our rickshaws and rode up to the North City. Lao Tai-tai always scolded me for not taking more people with me; I had therefore asked another friend to go with us. We made the rounds of the courtyards and houses that were now so familiar to me. I saw them through my own accustomed eyes, but I saw them also through the eyes of my friend, to whom the Japanese gardens were the most beautiful in the world, and knew that Lao Tai-tai's were good. The early summer flowers were in bloom. The maze garden in the bamboo court was a blaze of color from the early-blooming annuals. At last I saw the Second Master's peonies in full bloom— great rose-colored blossoms, maroon or white. Their satin petals were marred, however, by the dust of a light wind. The summer rains had not yet come and the earth was dry.

"Too bad the wind blows today. The garden does not look as well as it should, and the dust gets into the eyes and hair and teeth." Lao Tai-tai was stating the obvious as all do when a point is to be made.

Back in Lao Tai-tai's room for the final visit and the confection of the Eight Precious Things, cooked by the new maid as well as ever by Ho Chieh, Lao Tai-tai apologized. "It's been a long time since I saw you—much too long. But I've been away. I've been in Tientsin." She hesitated a moment and then, having made her decision, said, "I was in Tientsin getting my burial clothes." She paused again and looked into our faces. "I couldn't find what I wanted here in Peking. The shops in Tientsin are much better, and the tailors, but even so I had to watch them stitch by stitch."

Neither of my friends could understand what Lao Tai-tai said. I would have to translate for them. Would they—Americans—be shocked by this preparation for death while still in life? Lao Tai-tai's eyes were asking this question also of me. I was not shocked. I knew that every man and woman tried to make ready all things needed before death came, many years before death, to have all in readiness before they started the long journey, all they would need when they set out to join the ancestors. The expression on my face was the one Lao Tai-tai wanted to see, and I felt sure also of my friends.

"Would you like to see my grave clothes? They are really beautiful."

"I most certainly would," I said. While she turned with her quick enthusiasm to the maid and told her to bring out the things, I explained to the others, who also had had enough experience in the old ways of the East to know that we were being treated as privileged friends.

"Come," said Lao Tai-tai, "come into my bedroom. There is no place here to spread them out."

The maid lifted the door curtain and we followed her into the room. I knew that the brass bed had long since been banished and the traditional kang, the bed of the Northern Chinese, put back. "This is much more comfortable," Lao Tai-tai had explained to me, not wanting to hurt my feelings by saying that the brass bed was not comfortable at all. "There is room to move around. The maid and I can spread our things around as we cut and sew. We can sit on the kang without danger of toppling over." And the way she sat, would want to sit, was with her legs crossed, in the position of Buddha on his Lotus Throne and of all Northern Chinese on their platform beds, their kangs, which were their living rooms as well as their beds.

The room was again the pleasant Chinese bedroom and living room. There was the chest of polished red wood with its heavy brass fittings against the wall near the kang; the high wardrobe of red wood, its round copper plates reflecting the sunshine, against the north wall; and the wide kang, built up of mud bricks and covered with kaoliang matting, filling more than the southern third of the room where the sunshine could pour on it through the lattice of the wide windows. "We sit here and sew, the maid and I." And I could see them, one on either side of the low table in the center of the kang, against the background of folded quilts piled high on low red-wood cabinets on either end of the bed. I looked at the bench-like cabinets with their many drawers and little doors into hidden sections where I knew Lao Tai-tai kept her toilet articles and all the little things that women use. There was a feeling of harmony and rightness in the room.

The maid disappeared into the further room, the one that had been the young daughter's room and had no door but the one into Lao Tai-tai's room. The maid came back with a light-weight black-lacquer trunk trimmed with gold designs. She laid it on the kang and then went back and brought out a pig-skin box, lacquered red.

With one of her quick movements Lao Tai-tai lifted the lid of the black box and then swept aside the cloth lying across the top—the cloth that must cover everything stored in Peking, even if in a container, because of the dust so fine it sifted through all the cracks. She lifted out the blue-cloth-wrapped parcels and laid them on the kang until the box was empty. She wanted to show us the things in the right order. She un-wrapped a parcel and lifted up a quilted pad such as Chinese lay on the kang when they are about to sleep. It was of red silk on top and blue cotton underneath. "This goes first into the coffin," she said, laying it across the kang at right angles to the window. "You see, the head must be toward the south and the feet toward the north."

Lao Tai-tai then took out the embroidered red silk sheet and spread it over the mattress, tucking in the sides. Again it was the way the bed where she slept was made every night.

"Here is the cushion for the head." Lao Tai-tai lifted the stiff white head-rest with its depression for the neck. It was covered with lotus flowers and lotus leaves, appliquéd upon it. It was like a rose-colored lotus flower itself, with green leaves and rose-colored buds. And there was a lotus flower creation like a tiny stocks that reminded me of the way our Pilgrim fathers used to shame their culprits. "Do you know what this is for? It is to keep the feet together—so they won't fly apart, so they will lie decently." She set it at the foot of the little made-up bed. Beside it she laid the tiny red shoes and white stockings.

A shadow had crossed Lao Tai-tai's face as she handled the foot-rest. It was the first thing that did not have a counterpart used in life. There are horrid tales in Chinese folklore of dead bodies rising and walking stiffly, stiffly out the door. No matter how much loved was the parent, the children must guard against any unwillingness of that parent to continue the long journey to the ancestors once the first step had been taken.

Lao Tai-tai turned back gaily to the bundles that had come out of the lacquer box. She took up the garments one by one. She was like a bride showing off her trousseau. She took up the red silk underwear—long trousers and short coat that would be next to the skin—like the white ones she was now wearing, or grey ones sometimes. The only difference was that instead of buttons these had cloth ties to fasten them. There were a pair of padded silk trousers and a knee-length padded coat to go on next. Then there were the formal pleated skirt of many colors and gay embroidery and the red silk formal coat, embroidered and banded with black satin, such as grand ladies wore on occasions of high ceremony. To go over all of these was the long, sleeveless coat, of embroidered black satin trimmed with a fringe, such as is seen often in the portraits of the Manchu empresses.

Again I thought of the pride with which every Chinese man and woman reflected that twice in their lifetime all Chinese had the right to be dressed as the emperor and empress dressed—once when they married and once when they were buried.

I thought also of the waste, of putting so much work and beauty into the earth to molder away. Perhaps they would not entirely disappear. Perhaps some archeologist, at some distant time, will find them, and the people of that time will know how people of Lao Tai-tai's time dressed as we now know how those of the Tang period dressed, from fabrics found in their graves as well as from pictures of the time. The beautiful workmanship was not wasted either. In a period when the agricultural-handicraft way of life was ceasing to be able to care for the people and the new mechanized-industrial way had not yet come in, it was useful to have the flourishing industry of making grave clothes to give a living to many families.

Lao Tai-tai pointed out the workmanship and the colors used in the embroideries—how carefully they had been chosen and matched to bring out the brilliance of the scenes pictured and of the birds and flowers. She lingered happily over the details. The men who did this work were highly skilled artisans.

Then there was the plain black silk coat to go over everything, to reach from her neck to a few inches above her ankles, the formal coat worn over everything when going out of one's home compound on ceremonial occasions. All other garments opened on the side. This one opened down the front.

Lao Tai-tai laid the garments one by one on the mattress in the order they would be worn. Then she laid the red-embroidered green-lined quilt of satin over all as though over a person in bed. Again she tucked in the the edges under the mattress pad.

"Then," she said, "this goes over everything, even over the head." And again I saw a fleeting shadow as she realized that her face would be covered and she would not be able to see or take part in the ceremonials, in the excitement around her. "You see," and her face was bright again, "this is the prayer robe."

It was a cotton cloth, large as a bedspread and of the Buddhistic holy orange-yellow color. The outline of a dagoba was printed on it, and in every space—in the dagoba and outside and around the edges—were printed prayers for the dead: that they might have a comfortable journey through the land of shadows, pass easily through the judgment halls, and reach the ancestors in peace. Though it was probably Nirvana and not the ancestors the prayers mentioned.

Lao Tai-tai was quiet as we looked at this "robe of a thousand prayers." It was as though she were thinking of that journey and wondering what it would be like, but there was in her no fear or hesitancy.

Then with a quick and radiant smile she told the maid to open the small lacquer box that had been lying beside the larger one. She took out a square glass case and set it on the chest by the bed. She lifted the glass case, though we could have seen through the panes. "This," she said, "is the headdress." She lifted the diadem such as one sees in the portraits of the empresses—gold filigree covered with kingfisher feathers, jade, coral, and pearls. Golden spirals ended in leaves green with kingfisher feathers and in red blossoms of coral and agate. Jade jewels and strings of pearls hung from the diadem. I could not tell whether they were real, as I strongly suspected, or imitation as in most burial costumes, for I would not touch the fragile, intricate, beautiful thing.

Lao Tai-tai held the diadem up for us to admire. "They say it is very becoming. I had to try it on when they were making it. But I can't put it on to show you. That would be bad luck." She held the dainty thing in her hand, and there flitted across her face the realization that she would not be able to enjoy how well she looked when she finally wore it. She smiled quickly. "But I can wear it on my seventieth birthday. I'll have my picture taken and give you each a copy."

Like a bride about to go to an unknown home, Lao Tai-tai had been showing us her trousseau for the last great journey into the unknown. Birth, marriage, death are but different turns of the same wheel. Each comes and takes its proper place.

We had walked for an hour in the garden of a soul nurtured and fulfilled and fulfilling a great tradition. We had looked into eternity.

CHAPTER 14

"I have not seen Lao Tai-tai for a long time," I said to Ho Chieh as she served my breakfast at the little table in the angle of the gallery by the elm tree. I had skimmed through the morning paper and found nothing of special interest.

"She has gone to Manchuria to see her brother."

"Has her Second Daughter a new baby?" I asked, knowing that this brother was the younger daughter's father-in-law.

"Oh, the daughter had her baby last year. Lao Tai-tai sees her often. There will be another baby in a few months. They live in Tientsin. The young man, her husband, is going to Nankai University. Lao Tai-tai went to Manchuria to see her brother. She had not seen him for many years. Even when she is in Tientsin she is busy looking up friends she has not seen for a long time." Ho Chieh seemed puzzled. "She is more active than she has been for many years. She is settling old accounts that have almost been forgotten. It is as though it were New Year time—only more so."

Ho Chieh was referring to the period at the end of every year when all accounts were settled, followed by the time when all friends were visited.

Then one day Lao Tai-tai came to see me unannounced, as was her way.

It was a still day in midsummer. The heaviest of the summer rains had passed and the earth was at its richest green. A group of us were waiting, that Sunday afternoon, in the big living room, since it was still too early in the day for us to sit in the courtyard.

We had planned an excursion, and the gathering place was my house. Some of the friends were in Peking but briefly, and this was the only time they had for this outing.

Philip, whom Lao Tai-tai had wanted for her granddaughter, was one of the party. Lao Tai-tai's face lighted up when she saw him. He came over and spoke to her before we introduced her to the other guests.

"You have a party." It was a statement and a question.

"We are taking these friends from America to dinner in the North Lake Park. We thought we would eat in the restaurant on the north side of the lake, the one where the Empress Dowager's cook makes wotou and tofu-paitsai."

Lao Tai-tai smiled. Everyone living in Peking smiled when this restaurant and the Empress Dowager were mentioned. The smile was always a compound of respect for the vagaries of human nature and of disrespect for the woman who had last sat on the Dragon Throne—not counting the little boy she had chosen in order to give herself a few more years of power and had left to sink with the empire. In the smile there was always the peculiar Peking indulgence which said, "She was a woman like us, and she had her ways as we have ours." In her lifetime she had given that easygoing gossip-loving city much to talk about. The old tales were sometimes still tossed around. Perhaps all the cooks who claimed to have cooked in her kitchen *had* cooked in her kitchen. She must have had many. But that Peking smile also said, "We know the commercial value of having cooked for the Empress Dowager, and we enjoy having our imaginations stimulated."

There was also the Chinese sense of the fitness of things in the fact that this restaurant, and several others besides, chose to sell, and the people to buy, of all the dishes the Empress Dowager had cooked in her kitchen, these common everyday dishes of the people, wotou and tofu-paitsai, steamed bread of the mixed grains, cornmeal and millet and soya beans, and bean curds cooked with cabbage.

In the Imperial Palace the table had been spread every day with every dish the Emperor or the Empress had ever touched: hundreds of dishes a meal. On occasion, from time to time, courageous censors took the Throne to task for such extravagance and told of the starving people. "They never, from the beginning of life to the end, even see such food as is daily left over on the Imperial Table."

"What do they eat?" the Empress Dowager is reported to have asked.

"The best they have is wotou and tofu-paitsai."

The Empress then ordered that these dishes be prepared for her, that she might know what the people ate. The imperial cooks then took the cornmeal and ground it fine instead of leaving it coarse as the people ate it. They mixed it with wheat flour. They made the tiny confections that looked like thumbs from yellow mittens, that had the sweetness of the corn and the smoothness of the wheat. They cooked the bean curd and cabbage with rare mushrooms and exotic spices so that the dish became one for gourmets.

"What is this you are trying to tell me?" the Empress was reported to have said. "Eating this—what have the people to complain of?" And who could tell the old woman that the people did not get even the undressed-up versions of tofu-paitsai and wotou as often as they would have liked or needed?

Everyone in Peking knew the Empress Dowager's family had been poor at one period in her youth. She had probably had a very good acquaintance with the nourishing power of bean curd, the people's meat, and of cabbage and corn bread. But no one let that spoil the story. Perhaps in those days even poor Manchus did not eat tofu-paitsai.

Lao Tai-tai smiled.

"And," said I, "we had planned to go first to the People's Market in the Lake of the Ten Weirs."

We all went often to the Parks of the Three Lakes that had been the Emperor's own gardens. At one of the huge red gates we would pay ten cents for a ticket and roam at our pleasure and for as long as we liked beside the lotus-filled water, under the old cedars, through the palaces and temples. But the people who did not have ten cents to spare also had their places to visit for recreation. There was the region by the Bridge of Heaven, where were the inexpensive tea houses and theaters, where the wrestlers and jugglers and story tellers performed in the open,

113

getting enough when the bowl was passed around to let them live on about the same standard as the people who came to see them. There was the open space paved with fieldstone around the huge white Bell Tower, where large square blue cloth shades, held up by central poles, made patterns in the sunshine. Under these shades the peddlers set their stands to sell soup and sweets and fruit to refresh the people who strolled along the streets and gathered there for amusement. Part of the amusement was seeing each other and part was being in a friendly crowd. During the summer months there was a fair at the Lake of the Ten Weirs to which the working people could go without entrance tickets, and also enjoy drinking tea beside the weeping willows, look at the red and the white lotus blossoms framed between the willows' drooping branches, against the background of palace roofs, and enjoy the water-cooled breezes carrying their fragrance. They could look at the graceful mass of the Drum Tower and enjoy its reflection in the water to the north, and to the south they could look at the White Dagoba rising above the red walls of the Imperial Palace Gardens and the green masses of the trees in the Parks of the Three Lakes. For a few coppers they also could drink Dragon-Well tea or jasmine-scented tea and crack watermelon seeds, or if they wished to have more substantial fare they could order wonton soup or a bowl of noodles.

"Good, I'll go with you," and I could see Lao Tai-tai already beginning to enjoy the outing.

Each of the eight or nine of us in the party had his own rickshaw. These were private rickshaws, rented by the month or owned by those who rode in them, and the rickshaw pullers were hired by the month. They therefore were not overworked and were well-fed. They were, or considered themselves to be, the aristocrats of the unskilled labor of the city, and put on airs. And never, if more than two or three of these were in a group, could they resist the urge to race, to show off their strength and dexterity, and also the style of their running. They also loved to turn corners. They seemed to feel that the more corners they turned, the shorter the distance; but I was sure they loved the sensation of control given them by turning the corners neatly and at as great a speed as they could, still keeping both wheels on the ground, or almost on the ground. I would not be surprised if among themselves this was one of the criteria by which they judged themselves. I often wondered how they could anticipate each other's actions quickly enough to avoid locking wheels or running the shafts of the rickshaws into each other's cars. Sometimes a rickshaw boy would leap into the air and swerve to one side when the rickshaw in front slowed suddenly, but I never saw a passenger spilled in any of these races, nor anyone hurt.

On this day the convoy of rickshaws whirled down the hutung to Hatamen Street, up that wide avenue and down another hutung, gathering speed rapidly. The little puffs of dirt raised by the padding feet of the rickshaw pullers settled again almost as soon as they rose, but enough dust climbed into the air to make those of us in the back rickshaws see as through a gauze veil.

Lao Tai-tai coughed the dust out of her throat. "They like to race, but it is dangerous, especially for one as old as I am," and she looked slightly apprehensive. A spill on the ground was not the kind of excitement she wished. I called to my rickshaw boy and asked him to stop racing and to ask the others to stop also. Gradually we persuaded them to settle into a steady run, and Lao Tai-tai's rickshaw boy whirled her to the front of the little procession where by precedence of age she belonged. Also her rickshaw puller had been proved to be the slowest in the group and was therefore made the pacemaker.

We stopped on the way, as we had planned, to see Charles Laughton in "The Private Lives of Henry VIII." Lao Tai-tai always claimed to be illiterate, but she read the Chinese captions flashed on the screen as fast as I could follow the speech and needed no translation from me. She followed the story without difficulty and enjoyed Charles Laughton's acting. She did not miss the implications of the story and added some of her own.

"Of course the Third Wife (Jane Seymour) had to die in childbirth. That was as it should be, had to be. She caused the death of the Second (Anne Boleyn). The wheel is just." Life was life whether in sixteenth-century England or China of that day.

"I like him," Lao Tai-tai summed up. I knew she meant Charles Laughton. We did not discuss Henry. He was in a pattern known to all dynasties.

We sped along Peichihtze, the paved way beside the stream that drained the Northern Lakes, the ones that first got the water from the Jade Fountain in the Western Hills.

By the massive red pike of the Drum Tower—the great building that the Emperor Yung Lo of the Ming Dynasty had raised in the city he rebuilt in the beginning of the fifteenth century—we turned west along the northern end of the Lake of the Ten Weirs. The rickshaw pullers drew us silently along the road between the weeping willows lining the lake shore and the series of long low buildings that had been, in Manchu times, the favorite restaurants of the princes. Even Emperors—slipping incognito out of the Forbidden City—were reputed to have come to them. Now the favorite places for the weddings of those among the people who could afford them, they were not at this time too expensive for ordinary middle-class people.

A broad curved avenue, bordered by willows, crossed the lake. In winter this curved avenue was a thoroughfare, but in the summer months it was a park for the people. There were tables shaded by matting and big blue cotton awnings like huge square beach umbrellas, and the stalls of those who sold soup and fruit and sweets were on either side. These stalls were built out into the lake and held up on stilts. A wide way was left between them where the people could stroll and walk, packed shoulder to shoulder.

We got out of our rickshaws at the northern end of this walk and told the rickshaw pullers to go on around the lake, to the south, to meet us at the North Gate of the North Sea Park, across the road from the southern end of the park we were in. We joined the throngs, some of whom were there just to see, some to buy the fresh water-chestnuts, the roots of the white lotus and the seeds of the red, and other fruits and delicacies. Many came to linger over their tea as they sat at the tables enjoying the breeze, the bustle, the crowds.

About halfway across we found a table and squeezed ourselves onto the three benches. There was no bench on the far side of the table: no one could be asked to sit with his back to the view. We watched the tea vendor pour boiling water over the Dragon-Well tea leaves we had asked for, pour it from a big copper kettle with a built-in stove beneath, fed by charcoal. We cracked watermelon seeds and ate peanuts, letting the shells fall on the planks and through the cracks into the water. We looked through the strands of the weeping willows to the west, where rice had been planted in the more shallow parts of the lake. The little paddy fields looked like the bright green patches in a huge patchwork quilt laid on the ground, the brown paths between the fields the strips that held them together. Beyond the paddy fields were the wide Entrance Terrace, paved with fieldstone, and the huge red green-roofed gate of one of the few Manchu princes who had been able to maintain his position and keep his palace.

The lotus, spread out in front of us and on either side, was not yet in full bloom, but we could see a few wide-open rose-colored blossoms standing among their big leaves, which still retained some of their fresh spring greenness and had not yet turned into the deep green of summer. Buds, looking like peaches on the ends of their long bare straight stems, stuck out of the water through the massed leaves moving gently in the slight breeze. It became a game to see who would first discover one of the white lotus blossoms, rarer than the rose-colored ones.

When we turned, we looked at the fresh faces of the young men and women, journeymen and their wives, clerks and those who served the needs of the people of the great city, the tailors, the shoemakers, the barbers, and the rickshaw pullers themselves, on their off days, all dressed in their best clothes, the gay reds and greens of the women and the blues and blacks of the men. Many of them carried long sticks of glacéed red-fruit, strung like beads on an abacus and waving like giant antennae. Floating over their sleek black heads were whirligigs of many-colored paper and kaoliang pith. These could be bought for a few coppers and clicked gaily as the people walked. They looked like butterflies fluttering over the crowd, and were carried, for the most part, by the children who walked, small replicas, by their parents' sides. We looked at the pleasant faces of the elders, happy to be out for an occasion they could enjoy with very little outlay of money. Over beyond the lake, through the willow veil, the green tiles of the Drum Tower looked black against the afternoon sky.

When the shadow of the Drum Tower began to stretch across the lake, the lotus to take on a golden tinge, and the edges of the leaves to look like old copper, we got up and started southward, out of this park without walls or gates, toward the North Gate of the North Sea Lake and our supper.

The walls that surrounded the Lake of the North Sea were red imperial walls. For eight centuries, and there had been other walls before, they had surrounded the lakes and gardens enjoyed only by the emperors and empresses, imperial concubines and ladies in waiting, and the eunuchs. Ten cents now gave anyone the right to feel withdrawn and exclusive, if that gave him satisfaction, or to luxuriate in the art of the great garden and to rest for a while from the world. The park did not seem enclosed, so artfully were the walls built and hidden by the low shrub-covered hills. Coming from the people's ancient playground to this that had been the emperor's and now belonged to the people was like moving from one to another of the eternal bends in the Everlasting Pattern. It was like leaving a bright open Yang garden for an enclosed Yin garden, also bright and open to the sky.

We walked along the north end of the North Sea, also willow-bordered, past old temples, to a grove of cedars. The little compound in the grove, with its walls, three houses, and courtyard, had become a restaurant. Perhaps originally it had been a tea house for the emperor, where he could rest and be refreshed if he became tired when looking at the lake or visiting one of the temples. We could have sat at a table in the main hall, we could have sat at a table in the courtyard, or we could have sat at one of the two or three tables under the trees, so spaced as to give each a sense of exclusiveness. We chose a table near the water and at right angles to the lake so all could look at the water, the lotus, and the White Dagoba on top of the palace-covered hill across the lake. Those facing west could also see the Five Dragon Pavilions, which seemed to float on the lake, their yellow and green glazed tile sparkling in the late-afternoon sunshine; and beyond them the Temple of Heaven and Hell, in which little clay figures climbed around and around a mountain reaching to the rafters, toward eternal peace, or fell over precipices to assorted forms of torture, shown realistically. Those facing east could see the red walls curving beyond the shore of the lake, the walls enclosing the grove of mulberry trees with the white marble altar in their midst where the empresses had worshiped the deities guarding the silk-worms, and the low red buildings where the worms had been kept. I wondered how many decades had passed since the last ceremonial. A row of fruit trees against the wall cast their short reflections into the water. Once I had seen them in bloom—red blossoms against the vermilion walls.

The young men of the party made much of Lao Tai-tai, as they had at each stage of the afternoon, and seated her in the place of honor. They put Philip beside her to translate for her and because they knew Lao Tai-tai liked him.

The waiter brought the menu to Philip as the only Chinese among the men. "Tell me what you want," he said, as he pre-pared to write down our choices on a slip of paper the waiter had given him. "Each one choose a dish."

This was a game always played. Each chose the dish he liked best. In this way variety was assured and the host knew the guests had what they wanted. If the dishes chosen did not make a balanced meal, the host, who had the last choice, could see that it was rounded out.

"Oh no," we all cried out. "We want the Empress's wotou and tofu-paitsai."

"Have to have more than that," Philip insisted.

"Lao Tai-tai chooses first."

And gaily Lao Tai-tai chose. But as soon as Philip's attention had turned to the waiter and was giving instructions, Lao Tai-tai got up. I rose and went to her.

"I must go home," she said.

"But we have not yet eaten."

"That is why," she said, walking toward the gate. "I had forgotten. This is one of the days I fast—eat no meat. I had forgotten. I must go home."

She would not listen to my polite and sincere suggestions that we get vegetarian dishes for her, which we could easily have done. In fact the tofu-paitsai itself was a vegetarian dish. The determination in her quick brisk step was strong. There was a shadow on her face that her forgetfulness of the day did not explain, and I did not think she had forgotten. It was an excuse for something else. There was a withdrawal I had never seen in her before. She was not shutting me out—her spirit had gone somewhere far away.

"Go back," she said. "Your guests await you. I can find my way. The rickshaw awaits me at the gate."

"I cannot do that, I must accompany you to the gate."

"Please go back."

I knew she had some reason I did not know to ask this favor of me. So I stopped and stood watching the straight little figure walk off between the cedars and the willows, into the deepening twilight.

CHAPTER 15

I was awakened one morning in the late autumn by Ho Chieh. The grey of morning had not yet begun to break into the blackness of night. I could barely make out her form as she stood in the doorway.

"Pu Chaoshih, Pu Chaoshih, it's Lao Tai-tai. She's very ill. The Second Master says will you send a doctor."

I had no telephone. The one in the hospital, on my desk, and the long legs of my rickshaw puller carried adequately all my messages. "How did the word come?" I asked.

"They sent a car for the doctor. It is waiting for your message."

"Then the chauffeur can go faster than any of us. I will write a letter to the chief of the Private Patients' Service. Tell the chauffeur to take it quickly. I will dress and come to the hospital right away." Even if they did not take Lao Tai-tai to the hospital, I could telephone from there and find out what was happening.

By the time I got to the hospital the doctor had been to see Lao Tai-tai. He had sent for the ambulance, and she was already in bed in the Private Patients' Pavilion.

"You'll find her on the third floor. Her son is with her. He is waiting to see you," the admitting officer told me.

A very solemn Second Master stood by her bed in the small first-class room. His face was grey, and his eyes were drawn.

Lao Tai-tai lay quietly on the bed and from time to time threw out an arm. She seemed to be asleep and looked very much as she always looked.

"They have given her morphine," he said. Then he came forward, and we went into the sun parlor, where we could talk without disturbing her, though it is doubtful if she would have heard us had we stayed, so deep was she under the influence of the drugs.

"She would not tell us she was ill. I have worried about her for some time, but she would not say a thing. Last night—this morning in the Fifth Watch—she began to vomit. We could not stop it." He sighed. "The doctor you sent gave her an injection, and then she stopped. He said we should bring her here for an examination, here where there are X-rays and tests and where they can watch her." The Second Master paused and looked out over the roofs of the city toward the east, where the sky was turning red. "I think the doctor knows what is the matter, and I think there is no hope."

"Oh," I said, "you mustn't say that."

He shook his head. "For a long time she has been getting ready. At first I wondered why she was settling all her accounts, many of them old and most of them forgotten; and calling on all her old friends, looking up friends she had not seen for years—thinking of every member of the family, making arrangements for each of us. You've seen the houses she was building for rent. She is building another set—for Little Root's education. She asked me to hurry the workmen. She wanted to see them rented, she said. Then she bought the grave clothes."

I nodded.

"She ordered her coffin taken out of the storehouse and had it polished."

"Oh," I said, "you must not give up that way."

He smiled, though with difficulty, and to encourage me. "I am not giving up. If the doctors can save her we will be grateful ten thousand years. It is that I think she knew her time is drawing near."

When the formalities for the stay in the hospital had been concluded and we stopped in to see Lao Tai-tai again, the Second Master took my hand, a thing he had never done before. "I leave her with you," he said and went away.

Day after day Ho Chieh sat by Lao Tai-tai's side. Having her old slave girl and companion with her seemed to quiet her. She seemed always to be in restless sleep and never opened her eyes.

The family came and went. Every day I talked with the Second Master either at the hospital or over the telephone. The Third Master came. The Fourth Master came all the way from Tientsin, and for the first time I saw him. Beside him the Second Master was small and the Third, though tall, seemed not to be there. The Fourth was one of the most beautiful men I had ever seen. He was as tall as the Third but not at all willowy. He was filled out and perfectly proportioned, as could be seen in the Western-style business suit he wore with style and practiced ease. His face was better proportioned than Lao Tai-tai's, and he was many times better looking than the Second Master, though in these three faces there was a strong similarity. Leashed arrogance seemed a more natural expression for that face than the still sorrow.

Several times every day I went to see Lao Tai-tai, but she was not conscious of the outside world. The hospital, steam-heated, felt hot to most of our patients. Lao Tai-tai tossed on the soft, hot bed, throwing off the covers. But perhaps it was not the heat of the bed that made her toss. It was hard to believe that in that body, smooth, round, and fresh as a young girl's, there was growing that which would take her from us. And the face—without the knowing eyes looking at us and but for the grey hair—might have been that of a young woman, smooth, unlined, and strong.

Then the Second Master came and took her home. The doctors had told him what they thought was the matter and asked if they might operate.

"Will an operation save her life?"

"Probably not, but it might prolong it awhile."

"In suffering?"

The doctor had no answer that was good to hear. "It would help to have the diagnosis confirmed."

"That is of no consequence. If we cannot save her life, we will not break her body." In this the Second Master was acting according to the ancient mores of the people, according to the deep conviction that the body must be returned whole to the ancestors as it had come from them. That he had been willing to consider an operation that would break into the body, if it would save his mother's life, showed him to be a true Chinese in his acceptance of fact and willingness to be practical. It also showed him to be a man of changing China, a China on its way into the modern world. "And we will not put her to that amount of discomfort."

The Second Master took her home, and she died without regaining consciousness.

They gave her a great funeral, as was fitting for the head of a great family. They took her and laid her beside the Old Master, in the place that had been prepared for her long before even he was buried.

They dressed her in her grave clothes. They set the crown on her head, the crown she had never worn in life, for she was only sixty-eight.

They laid her in the coffin with all the family around her, all but the eldest son, who was not her own and was sick at the old home in Anhwei Province, and the foreign woman who was the wife of the Fourth. She had stayed home in Tientsin and refused to come. The others—Lao Tai-tai's own three sons and two daughters, the two daughters-in-law and the two concubine daughters-in-law, and her grandsons and granddaughters—wept as they gathered around and saw her laid in the coffin.

For seven times seven days the monks chanted prayers for the smooth journeying of her soul.

Dressed in the unbleached sackcloth with sackcloth bands around their heads, her descendants knelt on the ground in the order in which they had joined her growing family. They wept as the coffin was raised and carried out. As the bearers lifted the coffin and placed it on the carrying frame, and as the Second Master, taking his place of the Eldest, which for Lao Tai-tai was his, broke the bowl; and as the steward set fire to the paper money and the incense, they all knelt on the stones of the court with their heads on the ground and wept for the mother they really loved, who had left them.

As the sixty-four bearers took her out of the home she loved so much and the monks chanted, her family wailed, and each wailed his own grief. The bitterest weeping of all was that of the Fourth Master, who wept with no woman behind him and no train of small white-clad figures. Alone he wept for the Fourth Branch of the Family, and alone he wept for himself and his love for his mother. And the weeping he made was, "Mother, oh my Mother, that I should have brought a strange woman into our home to plague you, to shorten your days among us."

AND AFTERWARDS

The Second Master came to see me and thank me for all I
had done.

It was polite of him, and it was the custom to thank all who
had helped in any way during the last illness and funeral. I had
done nothing. I would have done any amount if there had been
anything I could have done.

"We all loved her," was all I could say.

He would not obtrude his grief on others. He did not change
expression, but there was a barely perceptible tightening of his
face. I knew, however, what that meant.

"You were her friend. She loved to have you visit her and enjoy the garden with her," he said as he was taking his leave. "I
hope that you will bring your friends to see the gardens as you
did when my mother was with us."

I thanked him and promised, but I could not find it in my
heart to go when I knew my old friend was not there.

Then came the war. The city filled with Japanese civilians,
forerunners of their armies; and with Chinese refugees, country folk who had fled from their homes around which the armies were fighting, small-town folk whose villages had been
burned. Chinese matrons and women from over the seas
banded themselves together to raise money to feed the refugees. While talking over ways to raise this money someone
spoke of the gardens of the city, the gardens and courtyards
behind the tall grey-brick walls. They said that the tourists (the
city was full of the last tourists who were to visit it for almost
ten years) had seen Japanese gardens but never Chinese. They
would leave Peking thinking it was a city of grey walls and
dust. Then these men and women on the committee to raise

money, many years resident in Peking, said they themselves had never seen the gardens they had heard me speak about.

So I went around the city to my Chinese friends and asked them, in the name of the dispossessed, to open their private gardens, hidden behind the walls from all but their friends, to the curious from over the seas.

I asked the Second Master.

"Of course," he said. "My mother would be pleased."

I was glad there was a crowd with me as we went from court to court along the well-known circuit. I was glad I had to tell them about the gardens and the houses, to tell them about the chrysanthemum shows of the city and to wonder aloud if the Second Master planned to enter any of his plants in the show that autumn, so I would not have too much time to miss the upright little figure that used to walk before us with so much grace and vigor. I had time, however, to see that the figure walking before us, the Second Master taking his mother's place, leading us from court to court, was very much like hers, more so than I had ever before noticed. He walked with the same shoulder movements as she had walked, and his contours were a masculine version of hers. I saw that as the Second Master grew older he was becoming more like his mother as I had first known her.

Little Root, solemnly following a half step to the left and behind his father, dressed as his father was dressed in a long blue gown, was now a big boy of twelve. He was attending school and doing very well, his father said.

Little Root's mother had gone to Nanking to make the final arrangements for the marriage of his sister. She was a student in the women's college and was to marry a young man in the university, one she had picked herself.

His other children were all well also. We would see them when we got to the part of the compound where they lived. There were now four boys there and the little girl.

I thought he was going to skip the little courtyard with the shrines. But he detoured and took us through the Bamboo Court and back of the Rockery into the little Court of the Shrines.

He took us first into the little house on the left—the Ancestral Temple. "My mother's soul-seat is there." He pointed to the shrine house on the right. Lighting a bundle of incense, he placed it reverently before the tiny closed doors. I bowed before the tablet of my old friend.

He then led us across to the house on the right—the House of the Gods. As he opened the doors he looked at me and said, "I am now the Head of the Family, and I must have in this house that in which I believe."

He opened the doors. The walls were bare. Gone were the Buddhas and the Kuan Yin, the Master Fox and God of Learning. Opposite the door, in the place of honor, was a plain wooden tablet of larger than usual size. On the black lacquer were four Chinese ideographs in gold—Of High Heaven the Seat.

"I do not know," he said, "who is the Great God of the Universe, but I know there must be one, and He is the Great God I worship."

The Second Master lived in a time of shifting values and great uncertainties. He knew doubt and also the oneness of all human aspiration. His younger sister, his daughters, and his sons lived in a world in conflict where old barriers were breaking down, in an age of working, however creakingly, toward the brotherhood of all mankind. But Lao Tai-tai was the fulfillment of thousands of years of Chinese culture, and lived by faith in the family, a family that was extended, in both the privileges and the responsibilities of privilege, to all her friends. Each generation lived in the spirit of its age, striving with what the age had to offer for the best way of life the age could give.

The Second Master led us back through the formal gardens to the Great Gate and out through the Moon Gate. He did not take us to the Second Gate, the one flanked by the four tall trumpet trees. He was not taking us through Lao Tai-tai's own courtyard and house, and I was content. I knew I would not want to see those rooms without her there.

"I am not taking you through my mother's courtyard. I hope you do not mind. I am keeping it just as it was."

I knew he meant it was now a special shrine to her and to the Old Master, where incense was burned daily before their portraits. I could imagine that these portraits now stood on the table in the ceremonial bay opposite the door, and that on the first and the fifteenth of each month this son went into the court and into the house, offered incense and made obeisance before them.